The Particular Description of England. 1588.
With Views of Some of the Chief Towns and
Armorial Bearings of Nobles and Bishops

719 **Smith** (William, *Rouge Dragon*) THE PARTICULER DESCRIPTION OF ENGLAND, with the Portratures of Certaine of the Cheiffest Citties and Townes, 1588, from the MS in the Brit Mus, edited by Wheatley and Ashbee, *illuminated map and armorial title*, 17 *plates* (230 *coats*) *of arms of the nobles, sees, towns, etc., of England*, BEAUTIFULLY TINCTURED, *plans or bird's eye views of 15 cities, all highly* COLOURED 4°, *original half morocco*, *Subscribers only*, 1879

Most important to students of Elizabethan England, the plan of Bristol is dated 1588 and is probably the earliest Smith drew—as in other cases, it is also the earliest known. The herald actually visited and drew the towns, on the spot. His arms of the peers are historical, including all former holders of the titles

WILLIAM SMITH'S DESCRIPTION OF ENGLAND

250 COPIES

PRINTED FOR SUBSCRIBERS ONLY

FRONTISPIECE.

THE
PARTICULAR DESCRIPTION
OF
𝔈ngland.
1588

WITH VIEWS OF SOME OF THE CHIEF TOWNS AND
ARMORIAL BEARINGS OF NOBLES AND BISHOPS

BY
WILLIAM SMITH,
Rouge Dragon

EDITED, FROM THE ORIGINAL MS IN THE BRITISH MUSEUM,
WITH AN INTRODUCTION, BY HENRY B WHEATLEY, F S A
AND EDMUND W ASHBEE, F S A

London.
PRINTED FOR SUBSCRIBERS ONLY
MDCCCLXXIX

HERTFORD
PRINTED BY STEPHEN AUSTIN AND SONS

INTRODUCTION

THE book which is here reproduced appears to have been almost entirely overlooked, in spite of its unique interest. The early history of the MS is not known, but we learn from a note on the fly-leaf at the beginning of the book that it was given to Sir Hans Sloane by Sir Paul Methuen. It came into the possession of the nation when the British Museum was founded by the purchase of Sloane's Collections.

The Manuscript is mentioned by Noble in his History of the College of Arms, who says, "He (Smith) wrote a description of this kingdom embellishing it with drawings of its chief towns" (p 218).

It may seem strange to some that a work containing carefully drawn views of London, Cambridge, Bristol, Bath, &c, made in Elizabeth's reign, should not have attracted notice, but nothing will surprise those who know what treasures lie hidden in the MS collections of our country.

In 1876, when one of us (H B W) was compiling a notice of Norden's Map of London for Mr Furnivall's edition of Harrison's Description of England (New Shakspere Society), his attention was drawn by Mr Furnivall to a note in Rye's Foreigners in England, where mention was made of the view of London. The MS was then examined and its value at once seen. Mr Furnivall caused woodcuts to be made of the views of Canterbury and Cambridge for publications of the Chaucer and Early English Text Society. We (Mr Ashbee and H B W) consulted on the best means of reproducing the book, and the former undertook to superintend the reproduction of the coloured plates.

A Prospectus was issued and subscribers' names received; but when the work was put in hand, it was found that more labour was necessary in the tracing of the views, etc, than was expected hence the delay in production. It is hoped that now the work is finished it will give satisfaction to those who have patronized the venture.

Permission to print the MS and facsimile the plates was obtained from the Trustees of the British Museum, through the kindness of Mr Bond, then Keeper of the Manuscripts, now Principal Librarian. The outlines of the views and arms are in exact facsimile, but it was not thought desirable to follow the rough colouring closely. The written portion has been printed exactly as it appears in the MS, contractions only being filled out in *italic*. These italics must not be confused with the names of places which are also printed in *italic* for the purpose of distinction.

The materials for the history of the author are not numerous, and they consist chiefly of notices of the work done by him, which was not inconsiderable. The names William Smith have been borne by so many men that it is not always easy to eliminate the facts relating to a particular one.

Our William Smith was a younger son of Randle Smith, of Oldhaugh, in the parish of Warmincham, in Cheshire, and his wife, Jane, daughter to Ralph Bostock, of Norcroft in the same County. The Smiths of Oldhaugh were a numerous and respectable family who sprang from the house of Smith of Cuerdley, Co. Lancaster, and bore the same Arms with a crescent for difference. We do not know when William Smith was born, but from other facts we may fix the date as somewhere about the year 1550. He appears to have been educated at Oxford, but Ant. a Wood was unable to find out to which house he was attached. Wood thinks it probable that he studied at Brasenose, and as that College was founded by a collateral ancestor, this is highly probable. Wood writes: "One Will. Smyth was admitted bach. of arts 8 Feb. 1566, another Will. Smith was admitted to that degree 15 Oct 1568, being the same, as it seems, who was admitted of that faculty 17 May 1572. And another Will. Smith was admitted bach. 10 of June 1572, but whether either of these was the author I am now speaking of, I cannot tell."

The first authentic date which we have to guide us in our researches into the history of William Smith is the death of his mother in March, 1561-2. Six years afterwards, he visited Bristol, as appears by the inscription attached to the view of that town in this book, which is as follows: "Measur'd and laid in platform by me Wm Smith at my being at Bristow the 30 & 31 of July An Dm 1568."

For some years we lose sight of Smith, and as we know that he settled for a time in Nuremberg, it is fair to believe that he was there in 1578, when he wrote his *Genealogies of the Different Potentates of Europe*, 1578. This MS formerly belonged to Peter Le Neve, and is now among the Rawlinson MSS in the Bodleian Library.

If, however, the date given by Brydges, in the *British Bibliographer*, to a MS of the Description of London be correct, Smith was a citizen of London and member of the Haberdashers' Company as early as 1575.

There were many Smiths in Germany, and our William may have gone over there at the invitation of some kinsmen. He kept an inn at Nuremburg with the sign of the Goose, and about 1580 he married Veronica, daughter of Francis Altensteg, of that place, and in the same year he drew up his *Angliæ Descriptio*, which is dedicated to Christopher Thurer. In 1581 his first child William was born, and in the following year he wrote a small tract, entitled, "How Germany is devyded." This is stated to have been written at Nuremburg on the 20 Dec 1582. In 1583 his daughter Jane was born, and in 1584 he wrote a little book of 76 leaves entitled, "The Armes & Discent of the Dukes, &c."

INTRODUCTION

On 6 Oct 1584, his father, Randle Smith, of Oldhaugh, died, and it seems probable that about this time William returned to England, which he does not appear to have left again, although he is sometimes styled, for purposes of identification, Smith of Nuremburg. In 1585 he was in Cheshire, and in his Treatise on the History and Antiquities of Cheshire in 1588, are views of Chester signed and dated Sept 7, 1585, and a large coloured map of the county, dated Sept 9, 1585. In 1586 his daughter Frances was born, and in the same year he compiled *The Image of Heraldry*, which is among the Rawlinson MSS. In 1587 he produced his first *Baronagium*, and about this time he must have been occupied with the Description of England, for the plan of Canterbury is dated "Oct 10, 1588," and the title-page of the book contains the same date, which is the year attached to the Description of London, a MS of which is also in the British Museum.

In Brydges' *British Bibliographer* (vol 1 p 539) there is a notice of an earlier edition of this book, dated 1575, in which the lists of mayors and sheriffs are continued by another hand as late as 1633. Added to this is the XII Worshipfull Companies, dated 1605, another copy of which is in the Bodleian Library and was or is to be issued in facsimile by Messrs Price & Co.

This last work is imperfect, as appears by the following note. 'These be all [the arms] that be yet come to my handes. If any desyre to know who were the rest lett hym spend but half so much tyme in searching for them (as I have done for these), and he shall either light on them or ells not find them at all".[1]

In the same year (1588) he prepared a copy of his "Vale Royal of England" and his son Paul was born. In 1590 his daughter Hester was born, and about 1594 he prepared his Description of Noremberg, which is now in the Archbishop of Canterbury's Library at Lambeth Palace. In 1597 he produced another *Baronagium Angliæ*, and also a small MS "Names of all the Knights &c."

Early in life Smith seems to have turned his attention to Heraldry and Genealogy, and he evidently long looked forward to obtaining a footing in the College of Arms,—with this object he made friends. On October 23, 1597, he was created Rouge Dragon Pursuivant, an office for which, according to Noble, he was a suitor for two years. He was recommended by Sir George Carey, Knight Marshal, and by many officers of the College. "The Society of Arms, finding by many that he was honest and of a quiet conversation and well-languaged, joined in the supplication, signed by Dethick, Garter, Lee, Clarenceux, Paddy, Lancaster, Segar, Somerset, Thomas, Chester, Brooke, York, Raven, Rouge Croix, Lant, Portcullis, and Treswell, Blue Mantle. So respectable a recommendation gained him this office".[2] In an abstract of James the First's revenue, etc, attached to *Truth brought to light*, which contains the fees of the Heralds and Pursuivants, occurs the following entry. "To William Smith, alias Rougedragon, £10."

He never rose to any higher office, and this may have been the result of the

---

[1] British Bibliographer, vol 1 p 543
[2] Noble's History of the College of Arms, 1805, p 217

ill-nature which made him prone to say disagreeable things of his fellow officers.[1] But in spite of this fault he appears to have been thought well of. Wood says that Camden had a respect for him, from which fact he draws the just inference that Smith must have been eminent in his profession. Between the years 1598 and 1605 he appears to have been busily occupied in his heraldic undertakings. In 1607 he accompanied Sir Gilbert Dethick, Garter, to France in attendance on the ambassador, the Marquis of Northampton. From this date to the time of his death we have little or nothing to record. He died on the 1st October 1618, and Wood is of opinion that he was buried in the churchyard of St Benedict, near Paul's Wharf, in which parish part of the College of Arms is situated, but the registers of this church do not commence before the following year.

A few remarks only will be required upon the book which is here produced. Although the date, 1588, and the Royal Arms of Elizabeth with the initials "E R," are on the title-page, there is internal evidence to show that the book was not completed until the reign of James. Thus on page 9 is a list of "Manor places belonging to the King," and on page 25, Hampton Court is described as "the fayrest howse that the king hath." Part of the book, however, was evidently written previous to the date on the title, as may be seen from allusions to the Queen, and from the fact that, on page 37, Kenilworth is said to be in the possession of the Earl of Leicester, who died in 1588.

The coloured Plates, which consist of Coats of Arms and views of towns, are very carefully drawn, and do great credit to Smith's skill. There are Arms of the chief towns, of Archbishops and Bishops, and of the chief noble families, arranged under the titles they have possessed. These Arms are spread about the MS, but it has been found necessary to gather them together upon separate pages, and their position is marked in the letterpress.

The views consist of profile sketches of Chester, Colchester, Coventry, Lichfield, Oxford, Salisbury, Stafford, and Winchester, which are of little topographical value, and bird's-eye views of London, Bath, Bristol, Cambridge, Canterbury, Norwich and Rochester, which are of the greatest interest. It appears to have been Smith's intention to give views of the chief cities (as his title implies), but he was forced to leave many spaces vacant for plans which he never obtained. Bristol is dated 1568, and Salisbury and Canterbury, 1588. Bristol, as he tells us was planned by himself. This town has always been one of great importance, and has found several delineators. One of the earliest views of the place was taken about the year 1479,[2] and Ames[3] mentions a map by Geo Hoefnagel, dated 1575.

Smith appears to have copied the plans of such cities as he could find to his hand, and only himself to have done those that he could not obtain otherwise

---

[1] See Noble, p 218. "Sir Christopher Barker, Garter (Henry VIII) Smith, Rouge Dragon, who was not deemed fit to speak well of his own, pretended to say his duties were not great, but he could only have it from hearsay, and the order can at times make to him refutes the calumny. — Noble, p 142. "Smith, Rouge Dragon, said that neither he (Richard Lee, Clarenceux, 1594), nor Cooke could write or speak true Latin, true French or true English."— Noble, p 171.

See Ricart's Kalendar, Camden Society, 1872. [3] History of Printing, p 538

The view of Cambridge seems to be taken from that by Richard Lyne from the work of Caius, edited by Archbishop Parker (De Antiquitate Cantabrigiensis Academiæ libri duo, Londini, J Day, 1574) This very rare view is much larger than Smith's, and if the two were not taken from a common original, there can be little doubt that Smith reduced and slightly altered the work of Lyne Ralph Agas, the supposed author of the Map of London, published a plan of Cambridge, three feet by four feet, but no copy is now known to exist Walpole fixes its date at about 1578, and Ames at 1589

In the Crace Collection of London Maps, etc, exhibited at South Kensington, is "A view of Old London copyd from an ancient Drawing" (No 374), said to be by William Stuckley, the original being "supposed to be by Anthony von Finden, 1560" The view is signed W S f, which initials would do as well for William Smith as for William Stuckley The two views are identical

As the early Maps of London are so few, one that has been unregistered hitherto cannot but be of the greatest interest The north bank of the river in this view is rather confused, but the churches appear to be drawn with care, and the various landing stairs and wharves are well represented The Palace of Whitehall and Westminster Abbey are laid down very clearly, but the distinguishing feature of the view is the space devoted to Southwark, Bankside, and Lambeth, in the foreground of the picture

The relative importance of the various towns and cities is shown by the size of the different views, thus most of the places are well represented in single leaves, Norwich is a double leaf, and London is folded into three Of York, the second city in the kingdom at the time this book was written, there is no view

In passing from a notice of the plans to that of the letterpress, it may be remarked, that although there is nothing of any great importance in the *Description*, yet the information is given in a racy manner, and the interesting points are numerous Huntingdonshire is said to be "four-cornered lyke a diamond uppon a payre of cardes," and of the Isle of Wight, we are told that "in forme it representeth an egg" We learn from the account of Bristol that "there is no dunghill in all the cittie, nor any sinck that cometh from any howse, but all convaid under the ground, neither use they any cartes in their streetes, but all sleades" (p 34)

"Bromicham (comonly called Bermicham) is a proper towne, with a high spyre steple, where great store of knyves are made, ffor almost all the townes men are cutlers or smithes" (p 38)

Of Chester, we read, "The howses are builded in such sort, that a man may go from one place of the cittie to another and never come into the streetes, which manner of building I have not hard of in any other place of Christendome" (p 44-45)

"York is the greatest cittie in all England next to London, which for greatnes & scituation (as some wryte) may be compared to Rome, as I have hard Winchester compared for scituation to Jerusalem" (p 47)

Smith gives a list of what he considers to be the seven wonders of England, and

b

adds London as the eighth (p. 6). He is also careful to give lists of castles, forests, and moors in the various counties.

The total number of members in the Commons' House when Smith compiled his text was 439, made up as follows: Knights 90, Citizens 46, Burgesses 289, "Barons of the Portes" 14 (pp. 62-64.)

There is a full and curious list of the principal fairs held in England, from which it appears that one was held on Ash Wednesday at five different places, nine towns held their fair on Ascension Day, and on five Sundays fairs were held in various parts of the country, viz. first Sunday in Lent, third Sunday after Easter, Whit Sunday, Trinity Sunday, and Sunday after St. Bartholomew's Day.

The work is concluded with a list of highways from town to town, which is somewhat like the one in Harrison's Description of England, but differs in several particulars. The distances are the same in both, and this resemblance between the two opens up a very curious question respecting the relative length of the measured and the reckoned miles, which deserves more attention than has hitherto been directed to it. Dr. Pearson made some remarks on this point at the Annual Meeting of the Cambridge Antiquarian Society on the 28th May, 1879, and the following is a report of his views taken from *The Academy* —

"Many years ago, in opening Leland's *Itinerary*, composed about the year 1540, the writer found the distance from Cambridge to St. Neots given as twelve miles, it being actually seventeen. This led him to think that old English miles were longer than the present statute mile, and on consulting Holinshed a few months back, he found that all the distances given by that author differ from the modern measurement nearly in the same proportion. It is not easy to account for the discrepancy between the actual measured distances and the popular reckoning. Ogilvy, in 1675, recognises it, and without actually referring to Holinshed, specifies the difference between the two modes of estimating the distance from London to Berwick at one-third more than the old measure. Holinshed gives in his edition of 1577 a specimen measure of half an English foot, differing from the present statute measure by only the tenth of an inch, and adds a table of length identical with our own. He also gives another mode of reckoning a mile, by the turns of a waggon wheel, which would make a mile less than 1,700 yards. A Scotch mile is 1,978 yards, an Irish mile 2,240, and a common English mile of the sixteenth century must have been at least as long as the latter; but there is no trace of the English perch having ever been like the Irish one, seven yards instead of five and a half. Possibly the explanation may be this. A league of three miles may have (theoretically) represented an hour's walk. But as a man will generally make four miles in an hour, the popular estimation of considerable distances would underrate them in the proportion of four to three, which will answer very nearly to the acknowledged discrepancy in the recorded results."

This discrepancy in the lengths of the different miles is frequently found in writers of the seventeenth and eighteenth centuries, for instance, Evelyn describes his birth-place, Wotton in Surrey, as little more than twenty miles from London, while it is in fact a little more than twenty-six measured miles.

LIST OF WILLIAM SMITH'S WORKS

This list, although ample, must not be considered an exhaustive one, and it is not improbable that there may be other MSS. by Smith lying unknown or unnoticed in both public and private collections. Our best thanks are due to Mr G. E. Cokayne, F.S.A., Lancaster Herald, who has most kindly furnished us with information respecting Smith's MSS. in the College of Arms.

1579 Genealogical Tables of the Kings of England and Scotland and the Sovereigns of Europe, to the years 1578-9, with their arms in colours, by William Smith
On fol. 3 is the Author's motto painted in white capitals upon a black ground, "Silentio et spe." Belonged to Peter Le Neve in 1703. folio
Rawlinson MSS. B No. 141. Macray's Catalogue, p. 498

1580 1580 Angliæ Descriptio. Quæ paucis complectitur omnium in hac Regione prouinciarum nomina, situs, limites, et alia, quæ ad easdem cognoscendas sunt necessaria
Dedicated "Amplissimo Viro, D. Christophoro Fhurero, Reipub. Noribergenss Senatori Prudentiss." Signed "Wilhelmus Smith Anglus" and dated "XXVI° Aprilis An° 1580."
British Museum Add. MS. 10,620. Sm. 8vo. 24 leaves

1582 How Germany is deuyded into 10 Kreises, that is to say Circuites, And the names of all such Estates, as dwell in ech of them particulerly. Also the yearly Contribution that euery member of the Roman Empire payeth for deffence against the Turk, which contribution is called in their language Turkstewr. Written in Nurmberg, ye 20 Decemb. 1582. p W. S
This small 8vo manuscript consists of 20 leaves written within printed borders
B. M. Harl. MS. 994

1584 The Armes & Discents of all ye Dukes, Marquesses, Erles, Viscountes & Lordes, that haue bin created in England, since ye tyme of W. Conqueror, vntill this present yeare of our Lord, 1584
[Royal Arms in colours, with the motto "Semper Eadem"]
Elizabeth Dei Gratia Angliæ, Franciæ et Hiberniæ Regina, Fidei Defensatrix, &c
This manuscript occupies 76 leaves 4to. It is neatly written, and contains about 340 coloured Coats of Arms
B. M. Harl. MS. 6099

1585 The Vale Royall of England, or Countie Palatine of Chester, containing a geographicall description of the said countrey or shyre, with other things thereunto apartayning. Collected and written by Wm Smith, 1585. *Wm Smith Rouge Dragon*, 1597. Sm. 4to
A MS containing 121 leaves, which formerly belonged to Sir Robert Cotton, and was given by his son, Sir Thomas Cotton, to Roger Norton. This is the copy that was printed in 1656 and is fouled by the printer's hands. Elias Ashmole bought it from Morgan, the Arms-painter
Ashmolean MS. No. 763 (Oxford), Black's Catalogue, col. 383
Ant. à Wood gives the following description of the MS. "It begins with a catalogue of the kings of Mercia, and afterwards follows the description itself, beginning thus 'This County Palatine of Chester,' &c. It ends with

an alphabetical catalogue of the arms of the gentry of Cheshire, among which are the arms of this Will Smith, the author, of Oldhough, viz. parted per pale or, and gules, three Flower de Luces counterchanged of the Field (quartering those of Oldhough of Oldhough) with a cressant for a difference, to distinguish that family from the eldest or first house living at Cuerdley in Lancashire, where Sir Tho. Smith about that time lived. A copy of this book coming afterwards into the hands of Daniel King of Cheshire, was by him published in fol. at Lond. 1656, together with another book on the same subject, entit. also *The Vale Royal of England*, &c. pen'd by Will. Webb, sometimes a clerk in mayor's court at Chester."—Wood's *Athenæ Oxonienses*, ed. Bliss 1815, vol. ii coll. 233-4

1585 A Description of the Countie Pallatine of Chester, a work deserving to be better handled, but want of cunning in the author was the cause. Collected and sett down by W. Smith, citezen of Norembergh

> The list of mayors and sheriffs of Chester ends with the year 1585
> Contains coloured folding map of the county, two folding views of the city, and a small one of Haulton. The last page bears the arms of Bostock (with twelve quarterings), of Swenter, and of Smith (with crest and motto "Silentio et spe") marshalled with those of Altensteig. 4to
> Rawlinson MSS B No 282. Macray's Catalogue, p 579

1586 Another copy. Folio, in a volume containing other MSS
> Rawlinson MSS B No 283. Macray's Catalogue, p 582

Another copy in the Harleian Collection.—See 1588

1586 Various heraldic tracts and miscellanies, collected by William Smith, Rouge Dragon pursuivant, to which the following title is prefixed:—

> The Image of Heraldrye shewing divers secrett matters and secrettes touching Heraldrye wherein is described the true path-waye to obtaine that excellent science fitt for to be knowne and readde of all those whiche are desirous to searche therein. Written año Domini 1586 et anno regni Reginæ Elizabethæ vicesimo nono

> A collection of 28 pieces by various authors, which formerly belonged to Anstis, who has written the following note at the beginning. "This was wrote by William Smith, Rouge Dragon, a very industrious officer in the College of Arms, temp Eliz Reg."
> Rawlinson MSS B No 120. Macray's Catalogue, p 489

1587 Baronagium Angliæ Magnatum, scilicet, illius regni stemmata recentiora ad consanguinitates affinitatesq: per intermixta connubia discernendas delineata
> Adiectis unicuiq: familiæ peculiare suum ac gentile insigne simul cum timbro seu Crista, galea in ornamentum posito 1587
> This appears to be written by Smith
> Harl MS 806 folio

1588 A Brief Description of the famous Cittie of London, Capital Cittie of this Realme of England, &c. Ann' 1588
> In the Author's autograph
> Harl MS 6363 4to

1588 The Particuler Description of England, with Portratures of certaine of the cheiffest Citties and Townes
> B M Sloane MS No 2596

1588 A Treatise on the History and Antiquities of Cheshire in 1588
> This MS is by Smith, and has a large coloured Map of the County, signed and dated Sept 9, 1585, a coloured bird's-eye view of Chester, a long view of Chester, signed and dated Sept 7, 1585, two small sketches of Haulton town, and castle, and of Beeston Castle, and 126 Coats of Arms in trick
> Harl MS 1046, ff 122—168

LIST OF WILLIAM SMITH'S WORKS

1591 German Coats collected by William Smith, of London, during his abode in Germany 1591   folio
> [Philpot's Press, College of Arms, marked ".]

1594 (circa) "A brief description of the famous Cittie of Norenberg in High Germany," written by W Smith about the year 1594
> There are three dedicatory epistles addressed respectively to Sir George Carey, Knt Marshall of the Household, Captain and Governor of the Isle of Wight; to Edward Lord Zouch, Cantelope and St Maur; and to the Rt Hon Sir William Cecell Lord Burghley
> The MS contains arms, with maps of the city and territory of Nuremberg
> Lambeth MS No 508   Described in Kershaw's Art Treasures of the Lambeth Library, 1873 (p 86)

1597 The Names of all the Knights in England in every particular Shyre, that serued [in Scotland] in the time of K Edward the first   w*th* the Blason of their Armes
> Apparently in Smith's autograph   Eleven leaves, the last three of which contain various heraldic memorandums
> Harl 4628   Leaf 261 in pencil

1597 Baronagium Angliæ Magnatum scilicet illus- Regni Stemmata recentiora, ad Consanguinitates Affinitatesq3 per intermixta Connubia discernendas delineata Adiectis unicuiq3 familiæ peculiare suum ac gentile Insigne, simull cum timbro seu crista galea, in ornamento positis, 1597
> The above title is within an outline border, similar in design to the title-page of the "Description of England, 1588"
> The autograph "Wm Smith, Rougedragon," is on the 2nd fly-leaf
> Harl MS 1160   Sm folio

1598 The Visitacion of Lancashire &c   Made in Anno 1567 Añoq3 9° R Eliz
> Visitacio iste Lancastriæ, transcripta et augmentata fuit in An° 1598 p me Wm Smith (ats) Rougedragon Prosecutorem ad Arma
> This manuscript is in large folio, and has an ornamental title-page with coloured Coats of Arms, bearing the above title
> It contains a large coloured Map of Lancashire, which occupies a double page
> Harl MS 6159

1599 A Book of Miscellaneous Pedigrees, a° 1599 collected by Wm Smith, R D
> [Philpot's Press, College of Arms, marked ".]

1600 Stemmata Magnatum   Liber Guilielmi Smith, als Rougedragon, Prosecutoris ad Arma
> A fine MS of Pedigrees and Arms, written and painted by Smith, so entitled
> It has an ornamental coloured title-page containing in the centre, a full-length figure of a herald, bare-headed, and dressed in the tabard   (Qy Is it intended for a portrait?)   In the four corners are coloured coats of arms of Smith, Altensteig, Bostock, and Swerter   and on leaf 36 is a Map of England
> This MS afterwards belonged to J Philpot, Rougedragon
> Harl MS 6156   A large folio

1600 Orders for the Feast of Saint George   Written first by Rob Cooke, alias Clarencieulx King of Armes, who exercised the roome of Garter, durante sede vacante dicti Garterii 1585   Transcript [et magnopere augmentatus] per W Smith, alias Rougedragon, Anno Domini 1600
> Copied from a "MS in 4° penes Ed Walker, mil"
> Ashmolean MS No 1108 (49a 58-77)   Black's Catalogue, col 727

1602 The Book of Coates & Creasts   Promptuarium Armorum   Begonne the 28 of May 1602   P Wm Smith Rougdragon
> In this MS on f 73 Smith gives the Arms of Rafe Smith, of Oldhaugh in Cheshire, which are identical with his own   They are the same as those of Sir Thos Smith, of Cuerdley in Lancashire, quartered with those of Oldhaugh
> Harl MS 5807   folio

1604 A large Alphabet in Blazon, beginning with the letter B

> "This is said to have been copied by William Smith, Rouge Dragon aforesaid, A.D. 1604, and perhaps may be the foundation of his larger Alphabet, of which a fair transcript is now at Wimpole."
> It is not written by Smith, but has additions by him
> B. M. Harl. MS. 2092, f. 20

1604 W. Smith's Alphabet of Arms

> "Finis p W. Smith Roughe (sic) Dragon 28 Jul 1604." Sm. folio, pp. 393
> MS. King's College, Cambridge, given to the College by Dr. Richard Roderick, of Christ Church, Oxford, brother of the Provost (Charles Roderick, 1689–1712).
> A transcript of this MS. was made by the Rev. William Cole, in 1744, which is now in the British Museum (Harl. MS. 5798).
> Brooke, Somerset Herald, states in his notice of W. Smith, that he saw this transcript in Cole's Library at Burnham, on 3rd May, 1777, and that "another copy is in my possession." This Ordinary by Smith and Philipot, a thin folio, is in the College of Arms, marked E. D. N., 72
> Harl. MS. 6184 was also a MS. of Smith's Alphabet, but this was missing out of the collection as early as 1824

1605 The XII Worshipfull Companies or Misteries of London, with the Armes of all of them that have bin L. Mayors for the space almost of 300 yeares of every Company pticularly. Also most part of the Sheriffes and Aldermen

> MS. Bodleian Library
> In Moule's *Bibliotheca Heraldica* (p. 104), mention is made of a MS. then, 1822, in the possession of T. Willement.

1612 The Visitation of Dorset-shire. Transcript p Wm. Smith, Rougedragon An° 1612

s. a. The Armes & Descents, of all the Kinges of England. Since the tyme it was named England (To say from K. Egbert the first Monarch therof) vntill our Soueraigne Lady, Queene Elizabeth

> What worldly wealth, what glorious state,
>   Can here on earth endure,
> But Death doth make an end therof,
>   To liuing wights most sure
> Only one thing doth florish still,
>   Though Dueil do disdaine,
> And that is Vertu which for ay,
>   Immortall shall remaine.—W. S.

> It consists of 22 leaves, and contains 43 coloured Coats of Arms
> B. M. Add. MS. 27,358
> In the Catalogue, and on the back, it is ascribed to Wm Segar, but this is a mistake, as it is really by Smith

s. a. Stemmata Varia. Folio. Contains many miscellaneous pedigrees written by Wm. Smith, Rouge Dragon

> [Philipot's Press, College of Arms, marked $^{16-10}_{5}$]

Rawlinson MS. B. No. 113 is a volume containing six MSS. viz. 1 Catalogue of the Kings of England. 2 Names of Dukes, &c. 3 Arms of Episcopal Sees, &c. Continued to the year 1634

> Some few insertions are written in red ink, to which the following memorandum, on a scrap inserted in the volume, appears to apply, "Smith, Rouge Dragon, the hand in red." Folio. Macray's Cat. p. 486

Harl. MS. 2221 (British Museum), which contains Arms of Bishops' Sees, Cities, Abbeys, Priories, 1591, is said to be by Smith, but does not appear to be so. A list in his autograph is inserted, headed "Abbeys, whose names are not in this booke"

In Harl MS 6601 are miscellaneous memorandums by Wm Smith, among which, on leaves 4b and 8b is the following list —

"THE TITLE OF ALL SUCH BOOKES, AS I HAUE MADE.

in folio Reg	Regum Principumq; Christiani orbis Terrarę ferè omnium genealogia
in Quarto	The armes & discents of all yᵉ Kings of England (since yᵉ tyme it was named England) to say from K Egbert the first monarch therof vntill oũ soueigne Lady Q Elizabeth
in quarto	The armes & discentes of all yᵉ Dukes, Marqueses, Erles, Viscounts & Lordes, that haue bin created in England since the tyme of W Conqueror, to say from the yeare of our Lord 1066 vntill this present yeare
in octauo	Brevis Angliæ Descriptio, Quæ paucis complectit omnium in hac Regione prouinciarę nomina, situs, limites, et alia, quæ ad easdem cognoscendas sunt necessaria
in 4°	A particular discription of all yᵉ Shyres in England wᵗʰ the portrature of yᵉ cheiffest Citties therein
in 4°	A description of the Roiall Cittie of London Capitall Cittie of this Realme of England
in 4°	The Vale Roiall of England or Countie Pallatine of Chester Contayning a geographicall description of yᵉ said Shyre or Countrey, wᵗʰ other thinges therto apartayning
in folio	How Germany is devided into X Circuites wᵗʰ the names & armes of euy pticuler member of yᵉ whole Romish Empire
in folio	A Booke of Sheildes & Healmes of yᵉ nobility & gentlemen in Germany
in 4°	A particuler description of yᵉ Cittie of Norimberg in Germany, wᶜʰ is accompted, & Right well worthy one of yᵉ goodliest Citties in Europe, wᵗʰ the order of the pollecey, rule, & goument of yᵉ same
	The Armes of the nobilyty & cheiffest gentlemen in Polonia
	Certaine mappes of Countreis & Citties"

LIST OF PLATES

⁎ *The names and titles in this list are given as they are in the original MS*

FRONTISPIECE—Map of England
ILLUMINATED TITLE-PAGE

PLATE I
Arms of London, Dover, Hastings, Kingston, Southampton, Exeter, Ipswich, Bedford, Northampton, Buckingham, Hereford, Worcester, Warwick, Duchy of Lancaster

PLATE II
Arms of York, Leicester, Lincoln, Bishopric of Durham, Nottingham, Shrewsbury, Lancaster, Isle of Man, Durham, Newcastle, Cheshire, York, Yorkshire

PLATE III
Arms of Archbishops and Bishops,—Canterbury, York, London, Winchester, Norwich, Ely, Worcester, Salisbury, Lincoln, Hereford, Lichfield and Coventry, Chichester, Bath and Wells, Exeter, Peterborough, Rochester, Gloucester, Bristol

PLATE IV
Arms of Bishops,—Oxford, St Davids, St Asaph, Llandaff, Bangor, Durham, Chester, Carlisle

Earls of Penbrook
1 Walter Gifford
2 Ric Strongbow
3 Wm Marshall
4 Wm Valence
5 John Hastings Erle of Penbrok
6 Wm De la poole Duke of Suffolk & Erle of Penbrok
7 Humfrey Duke of glocester, & Erle of Penbrok
8 Jasper Duke of Bedford, & Erle of Penbrooke
9 Wm Herbert
10 Wm Herbert

PLATE V
Erles of Kent
1 Tosty brother to K Harold Erle of Kent Beffore The Conquest
2 Odo Bishopp of Baieux half brother to Wm Conquerer, E of Kent
3 Hubert de Burgo Erle of Kent an° 1228
4 Edmund of Woodstock Sonne to K E I an 1328
5 Thomas Holland Erle of Kent, 1397
6 William Neuill L Faconbridge Erle of Kent an° 1444
7 The L gray of Ruthin now Erle of Kent

8 Roger Comin
9 Walden
10 Roger Mowbray
11 The L Percy now Erle of Northuberland

12 Rob Beamont
13 Simon Montford
14 Rob Ferrers
15 Edmund of Lancaster
16 Rob Dudley

PLATE VI
1 William Warren Erle Warren & Surrey
2 Hamelet Plantagenet Erle Warren & Surrey
3 John Plantagenet Erle Warren & Surrey
4 Thomas Holland Duke of Surrey & Erle of Kent
5 John Mowbray Erle Warren & Surrey

LIST OF PLATES.

6. The L. Howard Erle Warren & Surrey
7. Wm Fitzallen Erle of Arundell

Erles of Warwick
8. Turquen'l
9. Henry Newborow
10. John de Placentis
11. Wm Mandrul
12. Wm Beauchamp
13. Ric Nevill
14. Edward Plantagenet
15. Joh Sutton (alias) Dudley

PLATE VII
1. Reinold Erle of Bristow and Cornwall
2. Cador Erle of Cornwall beffore the Conquest
3. Richard Plantagenet Erle of Cornwall, & K of Romains
4. Piers Gaveston
5. John of Eltham
6, 7, 8. Edward Prince of Wales, Duke of Cornwall, Erle of Chester

Erles of Southampton
9. Stigand' Archb of Caterbury & Erle of Southampton
10. Wm Gibnon Erle of Southampton
11. Wm Fitz William Erle of Southampton
12. The L. Wriothesley Erle of Southampton

13. Hugh Beauchamp Baron of Bedford
14. Ingram Couney Erle of Bedford
15. John Duke of Bedford Regent of France
16. Jasper Duke of Bedford & Erle of Penbroke
17. The L. Russell, now Erle of Bedford

PLATE VIII
1. Camber King of Wales
2. Edward, Prince of Wales, &c
3. Lewillen Prince of Wales [true
4. Algart Erle of Chester & Coven-
5. „ „ „
6. Hugh Lupus
7. Hugh Kifchock
8. Ranulph Bohum
9. Edward Erle of Chester, Eldest Sonne to King Henry ye third

10, 11, 12. Edward Prince of Wales, Duke of Cornwall & Erle of Chester

Erles of Winchester
13. Clrton Erle of Winchester
14. Roger Quiney Erle of Winchester
15. Hugh Spencer, Erle of Winchester
16. The L. Grorthuse Erle of Winchester
17. Wm Pawlet Marques of Winchester & Erle of Wiltshire

PLATE IX
Erles of Lincolne
1. Wm Romare
2. Ranulph Erle of Chester & Lincolne
3. Rob Quincy
4. John Lacy
5. Henry of Bollinbrok
6. John De la Poole
7. Edward Clinton, now Erle
8. Ursons de obtot
9. Wm Beauchamp
10. Thom'l Percy
11. John L. Tiptoft
12. Wm L. Somerset, now Erle

Erles of Wiltshire
13. Wm Scrope
14. James Butler
15. Henry Stafford
16. Thom'l Bullen
17. Wm Pawlet

PLATE X
Erles of Essex
1. Wm Maundeville
2. Wm Say
3. Humfrey Bohun
4. Henry Bourchier
5. Thom'l Cromwell
6. Wm Parr
7. Walther Devereux

Erles of Northampton
8. Waldern, Erle of Northampton
9. Simon Longchamp
10. Wm Bohun
11. Thomas of Woodstock D of Gloc Erle of Buck Northaptō, & Essex
12. Wm Parr, Marques of Northampton

Erles of Salesbury
13 Wm Crispin
14 Wm Longespé
15 Wm Montacute
16 Ric Nevill
17 Margret Countess of Salesbury

PLATE XI
Erles of Devonshire
1 Armer Erle of Devon in ye Conquest tyme
2 Wm Courtney Erle of Devonshire
3 Wm Rivers Erle of Devonshire & Excester

4 John Beauford Marques Dorcet
5 Thomas Grey Marques Dorcet

6 Walter Constable Erle of Hereford
7 Humfrey Bohun Erle of Hereford
8 Henry of Bollinbroke Duke of Hereford
9 Walter Devereux, Viscount Hereford

Erles of Carlile
10 Marcatt Erle of Carlile
11 Ric D of Glocester & Erle of Carlile
12 Andrew Harklow Erle of Carlile

13 Edgar Adeling, Erle of Oxford
14 Edward Vere, now Erle of Oxford

15 Roger Montgomery Erle of Arundell & Shrewsbury
16 The L Talbot, now Erle of Shrewsbury

PLATE XII
1 Remold de Mohun Erle of Somerset
2 Edmund Beauford Duke of Somerset
3 Henry Fitzroy Duke of Richmond & Somerset
4 Edward Semer Duke of Somerset

5 Waldern Erle of Northumbland Huntington & Northampton
6 Henry Erle of Huntington, sonne to David K of Scotts

7 The L Hastings now Erle of Huntington
8 Wm Clinton Erle of Huntington
9 John Holland Erle of Huntington

Dukes of Norfolk
10 Thomas a Brotherton Erle of Norfolk, Sonne to K E I
11 Margret Segrave Duchess of Norfolk
12 Thomas Mowbray Duke of Norfolk
13 John Howard Duke of Norfolk

PLATE XIII
1 Edmund of Langley Duke of York & Erle of Cambridge
2 Richard (sonne to ye said Edmund) Erle of Cambridge

3 Robert Stafford Erle of Stafford
4 Humfrey Stafford Duke of Buckingham & Erle of Stafford

5 Walter Gifford Erle of Buckingham & Penbrook
6 Thomas of Woodstock Duke of Glocester & Erle of Buckingham
7 Humfrey Stafford Duke of Buckingham

Erles of Bath
8 Thurkill Erle of Bath In ye Conquest tyme
9 John Bourchier, now Erle of Bath

10 John Holland Duke of Excester and Erle of Huntington
11 Thomri Beauford Duke of Excester & Marques Dorcet
12 Henry Courtney Marques of Excester and Erle of Devon

13 Uttred de Raby Lrle of Westmerland
14 The L Nevill Erle of Westmerland

15 Raff, Erle of Estalnge & Norwich
16 Randulph Bigod Erle of Norwich

PLATE XIV
1 Edward Semer Erle of Hartford.

2 Remold Erle of Bristow & Cornwall

Erles of Darby
3 Walter Ferrers
4 Edmund of Lancaster
5 Henry L Stanley, now Earle of Darby
6 Henry of Lancaster

PLATE XV
Erles of Gloaster
1 Morviens
2 Wm Passy
3 Rob Fitzhamon
4 Rob Consull
5 Gilbart Clare
6 Piers Gaveston
7 Hugh Audley
8 Hugh Spencer
9 Thom^s of Woodstock Duke of Glocester
10 Humfrey Duke of Glocester
11 Richard Duke of Glocester

12 Roger Glanvile Erle of Suffolk
13 Robart Ufford Erle of Suffolk
14 Henry Gray Duke of Suffolk
15 William De la Poole Duke of Suffolk
16 Charles Brandon Duke of Suffolk

PLATE XVI
Erles of Nottingham
1 Wm Peverell
2 John Mowbray
3 Wm Barkley
4 Henry Fitz Roy

5 Cospatrick Erle of Cumberland
6 Raff Meschems Erle of Cumberland
7 The L. Clifford now Erle of Cumberland

Erles of Rutland
8 Edward Duke of Aumale, & Erle of Rutland

9 George Duke of Clarence & Erle of Rutland
10 Thomas Manners, now Erle of Rutland

11 Allen Fergant Erle of Brittain & Richmond
12 Joh of Gaunt E of Richm
13 Joh Brittain
14 Edmund Erle of Richmond & Margret his Wyff
15 Henry Fitz Roy Duke of Richmond, &c

PLATE XVII
Arms of Bostock, Swenter, Smith, and Altensteig

PLATE XVIII
Bird's-eye View of Canterbury (1588)

PLATE XIX
Bird's-eye View of Rochester

PLATE XX
Profile Sketches of Winchester and Colchester

PLATE XXI
Profile Sketch of Salisbury (1588) Bird's-eye View of Bath

PLATE XXII
View of Stonehenge Arms of Thomas Radcliffe, Earl of Sussex

PLATE XXIII
Bird's-eye View of Cambridge

PLATE XXIV
Profile Sketches of Chester, and Oxford

PLATE XXV
Bird's-eye View of Bristol (1568)

PLATE XXVI
Profile Sketches of Coventry, Lichfield and Stafford

PLATE XXVII
Bird's-eye View of Norwich

PLATE XXVIII
Bird's-eye View of London

*** *The Plates are printed in colours by Messrs Harrison & Sons, St Martin's Lane, Charing Cross*

THE
Particuler Description of
ENGLAND.
With the Portratures of
Certaine of the Cheiffest
Citties & Townes.
1588.

The Prologue.

HOW ENGLAND TOOK NAME

*Some wryters affirme that this land was first named Samothe, by Samothe, *[leaf 3] otherwise called Dis, the sonne of Japheth, and afterwards called Albion, by Albion, the sonne of Neptune. Which name yt kept vntill *the* coming of Brute, who (after that he had overcome the giantes which then did inhabit it) did name all the land Brutain, or Britain, after his owne name. And the people therof were called Brittains, which Brittains enioyed *the* whole land, & kept it in their owne posession, vntill such tyme as they were overcome of the Romains, vnto whom they became tributary. Not long after, the Scottes and *the* Pictes invaded *the* north part of the land, with whom the Brittains had many battaills. But being at last sore oppressed with them, and disapointed of the Romains of helpe, were forced to entertayne the Saxons & Englishmen, which were then roving vppon the seas, to seeke their adventure. For in those daies Saxonia *was much greater then it is now, ffor it contained *[leaf 3] Saxonia, Thuringia, Hessen, Braunswik, Luneburg, Holft, & Friesland, even to the very sea. It appeareth also by wryters that there came in at that tyme seaven sundry strange nations into Brittaine. But the cheiffest were Saxons, Englishmen & Jutes, who coming to helpe the Britains against their enemies, did, in the end, turne their weapons against their maisters w*hich* entertayned them, dryving them to the vttermost corners of the land, namely into Wales, Cornwall, & Galloway. And called *the* said Brittains, Walshmen, that is to say, Strangemen, as they be called at this day. Lyke as the Germains do vse to call the Italians bordering vppon them Walshers, & Italy they call Walshland, even so did the Saxons & Englishmen call the Britains Walshmen, & their countrey Wales, ffor before that tyme Wales was called Cambria. The Saxons, then Englishmen, having gotten sure posession of most part of the land, did send for more of their countreymen, which passing the seas, came over, & joyning them selves together, devyded so much of the land as they had gotten into seaven kingdomes, to say, Kent, Southsaxons or Sussex, *Est Saxons *[leaf 4] or Essex, West Saxons, March, Estengland & Northumberland, which Northumberland was after devyded into two kingdomes, namely, Deira, & Bernicia. But in the end the kingdome of West Saxons subdewed all the other. So that Egbert king therof (having brought all to one monarchy) comaunded all the land to be called England, & the people Englishmen, because he hym selff was come of the Englishmen. And king Alfred (which shortly after succeeded hym) did devyde *the* same into shyres. But to retorne to *the*

Britains or Walshmen. They, seing them selves thus to be overcome, and dryven out of their owne land, and knowing the Danes to be ancient enemies to the Saxons, did provoke the said Danes to enter the land, to be revenged on them, which Danes, after many bloudy battaills, (partly by matching in marriage with the bloud Roiall, & partly with force), did in the end gett posession of the crowne, which their kings enioyed for the space of xxvj yeares. During which tyme the Danes vsed great cruelty towards the Englishmen, but at the last they were all slaine in one night as our cronicles report, & the Danish wryters them selves do not deny. The Brittans or Walshmen (althowgh they were made tributaries to the Englishmen) yet had they alwaies their owne peculier Prince, vntill the yeare of our Lord 1282, that King Edward the First envaded them on ech syde, both by sea & by land, and with force overcame them, & slew their Prince named Lewillen. Since which tyme they have had for their Prince the King of Englands eldest sonne, who the very day of his birth, is called Prince of Wales, Duke of Cornwall, and Erle of Chester.

[leaf 4b]

[leaf 5 is occupied by the map — see Frontispiece]

A DESCRIPTION OF ENGLAND

[leaf 6]

Britaine, which at this day contayneth two severall kingdomes, & by two sundry names is called England & Scotland, is seituate in ye Occeane Sea, right against France. The greater part therof (lying towards the south) is called England, wherof only at this present I purpose to entreat, together with the Principallyty of Wales, the Duchy of Cornwall, & County Pallatyne of Chester. The length of this realme of England is, from Portsmouth in the south, to Barwik in the north, about 340 myles. The breadth, from Douer in the est to the Land's End in Cornwall, being west, about 320. And so being 3 cornerd I make it to be from Barwik to Douer 300 myles, from Douer to St Buriens in Cornwall, 300, & from thence to Barwik, 400, which maketh the compass round about to be 1000 myles. In which kingdome I ffynd to be 53 shyres, or countries, to say, 40 in England, & 13 in Wales, about 100 walled townes, 616 market townes, that is 560 in England, & 56 in Wales, and about 10,581 parish churches, to say, 9610 in England, & 971 in Wales. The names of the sayd shyres do ffollow.

The length & bredth of England.

Shyres, Cities, Walled Townes, & Parish Churches.

[leaf 6b]

SHYRES IN ENGLAND

1. *Kent*, whose cheiffe cittie is Canterbury
2. *Sussex*, which hath the cittie of Chichester
3. *Surrey* hath Southward, & in tymes past Gilford
4. *Hamshire*, wherein is the cittie of Winchester, but the shyre towne is Southampton
5. *Barkshire* hath Reding & Wallingford
6. *Wiltshire* taketh name of Wilton, in tymes a ffamous cittie, but now Salesbury, 2 myles thence, is the cheiffest
7. *Dorcetshire* hathe the towne of Dorchester
8. *Somersetshire* hath Bath & Welles, & a good part of Bristow
9. *Devonshire*, whose cheiff cittie is Execester
10. *Cornwall*, whose shyre town is Launston, but the greatest towne is Bodman, and the cheiffest towne of trafink is Truro
11. *Essex* hath Colchester, but the sessions are kept at Chelmsford
12. *Mullsex*, wherein is the famous cittie of London, & hard by it Westminster, newly made a cittie also

DESCRIPTION OF ENGLAND.

13. *Hartfordshire*, wherein is Hartford & St. Albons.
14. *Suffolk* hath Ypswich & Bury.
15. *Norfolk* hath the cittie of Norwich.
16. *Cambridgshire*, wherin is the Vniversity of Cambridge, & the citty of Ely.
17. *Huntingtonshire* hath the towne of Huntington.
18. *Bedfordshire*, wherein is the towne of Bedford.
19. *Northamptonshire* hath Northampton, & Peterborow citty.
20. *Buckinghamshire*, whose cheiff towne is Buckingham.
21. *Oxfordshire*, wherein is *the* Vniversyty & cittie of Oxford.
22. * *Glocestershire* hath *the* cittie of Glocester.　　　　　　　　　　　　*[leaf 7.]
23. *Herefordshire*, wherin is *the* cittie of Hereford.
24. *Worcestershire*, whose cheiff cittie is Worcester.
25. *Warwikshire*, wherein is *the* cittie of Coventrie, and the towne of Warwik.
26. *Leicestershire*, whose cheiffe cittie is Leicester.
27. *Rutland*, whose shyre towne is Okeham.
28. *Lincolneshire* hath the cittie of Lincolne.
29. *Nottinghamshire*, wherein is *the* ffyne towne of Nottingham.
30. *Darbyshire* hathe the towne of Darby.
31. *Staffordshyre* hath Stafford, & *the* city of Lichfeld.
32. *Shropshyre*, wherein is the brave towne of Shrewsbury.
33. *Cheshire* hathe *the* ffamous cittie of Chester.
34. *Lancashire*, whose shyre towne is Lancaster.
35. *Yorkshyre*, wherein is *the* great & ancient citty of York.
36. *Durham* is both a bishopprick & a county pallatine, taking name of *the* cittie of Durham.
37. *Westmerland*, whose shyre towne is Appleby.
38. *Richmondshire* hath *the* towne of Richmond.
39. *Cumberland*, wherein is *the* citty of Carlile.
40. *Northumberland*, whose cheiff towne is Newcastle vppon Tyne.

Hereafter ffolloweth the names of the shyres in Wales.

*SHYRES IN WALES. 　　　　　　　　　　　　*[leaf 7b.]

South Wales.
- *Monmouthshyre* seweth all writtes out of *the* High Court of Chauncery, at London, as other Shyres in England do.
- *Glamorganshire. Brecknockshire. Radnorshire.* } These 3 are named Southwales, and do sue their writts out of *the* Excheker at . . . . . .
- *Carmardenshire. Cardiganshire. Penbrokshire.* } These 3 are Westwales, & do sue their writts out of the Excheker at . . . . . .

North Wales.
- *Merinothshire. Anglisea. Carnaruanshire.* } These 3 are Northwales, and do sue their writts out of the Excheker at Carnaruan.
- *Montgomoryshire. Denbighshire. Flintshire.* } These 3 are Estwales, and do sue their writtes out of the Exchequer at Chester.

There is in England xxij Bishoppricks, & 4 in Wales, which is in all 26 (besydes one in *the* Ile of Man). The names of which Bishoppricks, with *the* armes of their Seas, I have placed hereafter.

[leaves 8*a*. 8*b*. and 9*a*. contain Arms of the Bishoprics of England: see Plates III. and IV. The following inscription occurs on leaf 9, after the arms of the Bishops of Durham, Chester, and Carlisle:—" These iij are vnder the Archbishopp of York, who is also a Primate of England, and was of long tyme Primate of Scotland also."]

*BISHOPPRICKS IN ENGLAND

These Bishopricks are by a Greek word called Diocesses, of which Diocesses
Canterbury hath Kent
Rochester hath part of Kent, but the Bishopp of Rochester is Almoner to the King
London hath Essex, Midlesex, & part of Hartfordshire
Chichester hath Sussex
Winchester hath Hamshire, Surrey, & ye Ile of Wight
Salesbury hath Wiltshire and Barkshire
Exceter hath Devonshire & Cornwall
Bath & Welles hath Somersetshire
Worcester hath Worcestershire & part of Warwikshire
Glocester hath Glocestershire
Hereford hath Herefordshire & part of Shropshire
Lichfeld & Coventry hath Staffordshire, Darbyshire, part of Warwikshire, & part of Shropshire
Lincolne hath Lincolnshire, Leicestershire, Bedfordshire, Huntingtonshire, Buckinghamshire, and the rest of Hartfordshire
Ely hath Cambridgeshire and the Ile of Ely
Oxford hath Oxfordshire
* *Norwich* hath Norfolk, Suffolk, & part of Cambridgeshire
Peterborow hath Northamptonshire and Rutland
Bristow hath Dorcetshire
St Davids, Landaff, St Assaph, Bangor. These 4 are in Wales, and have those suj shyres devyded amongst them which are in Wales, as in *the* description of Wales appeareth
York hath Yorkshire, Nottinghamshire, & a peece of Lincashire
Durham hath the Bishoppricke of Durham and Northumberland
Chester hath Cheshire, Richmondshire, most part of Lancashire, part of Denbighshire, & part of Flintshire
Carlile hath Cumberland & Westmerland

These 4, & that in the Ile of Man, are *the* province of the Archbishopp of York

*THE 4 PRINCIPALL RIUERS IN ENGLAND

Hereafter shalbe described the courses of the foure principall rivers in England to say the Thamise, Seuern, Humber & Trent (for the lesser shalbe spoken of in their places in the particuler description of every shyre) And first the Thamise

Thamise is first called *Isis, or Ise*, and springeth in Glocestershire, not farr from Cicter, and keping his course estwards, passeth through a corner of Wiltshire to Creklade, where it taketh in the river of Churn, *that* cometh from Cicter aforsaid, which is much bigger then it selff, and then passeth to Castleaton, Kemsford, & Lechlade, where it taketh in ye Colne, & beneath the towne the Lech, & so passeth to Ratcotbridge & Newbridge, where it taketh in a river called Windrush, *that* cometh from Whitney, in Oxfordshire, & after an other that cometh from Chippingnorton, arriveth lastly at Oxford, where (having receaved the river of Cherwell) passeth to Abington, and there receaveth a small river named Ock, which cometh out of Barkshire, and after at Dorchester meeteth with the river of *Tame*, becommeth navigable, altereth name, & is called *Thamise*, and passing to Wallingford & Reding where (having receaved in the river of Kenet) it torneth northest receiving by *the* way *the* river of Loddon, & so cometh to Henley devyding Oxfordshire from Barkshire all his course from Lechlade, a myle beneath Henley. From Henley the Thamise passeth to

Maidenhead, *Windsor, & Stanes, where it receaveth in the river of Colne, that •[leaf 11]
cometh from Vxbridge & Colbrok, and afterwards visiteth Oteland, where it
receaveth in the river that cometh from Gilford, & then Hampton Court, where
having received in the river that cometh from Coveham, it passeth a myle
thence to Kingston, where it is 500 foote broade, and then torneth northwards to
Richmond & Brainford, & from thence estwards agayne, arriveth at the noble
cittie of London, where it is 1000 foote brode. From London it passeth to
Deptfford & Grenewich, and at Blackwall receaveth ye river of Lee, that parteth
Essex from Midlesex, & after another that cometh from Barking in Essex, at
Wolwich becometh salt, & so passeth to Erith, receving by the way the river of
Darent (which cometh from Dartford), arryveth at Gravesend, & from thence (being
alwais broder & broder), nere to Ligh in Essex, having on that syde made
certaine small ylandes, cometh on the other syde to Quinborow Castell, in the Ile
of Shepey, where having received in the river of Medway, that cometh from
Rochester, is accompted there four myles brode, and having passed the sayd Ile,
it becommeth so broad (the land sayling on Essex syde) that it is accompted no
more the Thamise, but the meane sea.

*Severn (called in Latin Sabrina, & in Walsh Hauern, or Hafren), springeth •[leaf 11v]
in Wales, at a great hill called Plinlimon, at which mountain also springeth two
other rivers, namely, the Wy, & the Ridall. The Severn kepeth his course
northest to Newton, Montgomory, & Walsh Poole, after entreth into Shropshire
to Shrawden, but beffore it come there it receaveth in a river named Tanat.
After keping his course est, & sometymes southest, visyteth & almost en-
vironeth the fayre towne of Shrewsbury, and having received in the Terne at
Acham, passeth to Bildas, and Bridgenorth, bendeth somwhat towards the south,
cometh to Beaudeley in Worcestershire, & passeth through the said shyre to the
cittie of Worcester, where it receaveth the river of Teme, which cometh from
Ludlow, and so passeth to Vpton, & not farr from Tewksbury, in Glocestershire,
it receaveth in the Avon, which cometh from Warwik, & afterwards cometh to
the cittie of Glocester, & about 5 myles from thence, at Newnham, is salt water,
and beginneth to be very brode, and so ronning southwest, receaveth the river of
Wy, by meanes wherof yt becometh so brode (that after it hath received in the
Avon, which cometh from Bristow), it is then called the Severn Sea.

*Humber beareth only that name from the place where the Owse & Trent do •[leaf 12]
meet, vntill it come to the sea. The said river of Owse is greatly augmented by
the river of Swale, which coming from Richmond, meeteth with the greate river of
Youre, wherof York in old tyme did take name, by meanes wherof the Ouse
(which beffore was but a litle broke) becometh very great, & so receiving in the
river of Nid, arriveth at the cittie of York, & after meeteth with the Warf,
Derwent, & Acr, lastly with the Trent, & then is called Humber, & so passeth
to Kingstown, where it receiveth the river of Hull, and falleth into the sea at the
Spurnehead.

Trent springeth at the foot of Mowcopp Hill, which hill parteth Cheshire
from Staffordshire, and kepeth his course southest to Trentham & Stone, where,
not farr of, having received in the river of Sow that cometh from Stafford, it
becometh navigable, keping then his course estwards, passeth vnder Worsley
bridge & after receveth in the Blith, then Tame, which cometh from Tamworth,
cometh to Burton, after taketh in the Doue, then the Darwent, which cometh from
Darby, lastly the Sowre, which cometh from Leicester, passeth not farr from the
ffyne towne of Nottingham, and from thence northest & north to Suthwell &
Newark, then directly north to Gainsborow & Axxey, where it maketh an Iland
called Axholme, and after it hath received the river of Dan, that cometh from
Dancaster, meeteth together agayne, and so falleth or meeteth with the Owse,
and is called Humber, as afforsaid.

*WONDERS IN ENGLAND

It is said that there are vij wonders in England, lyke as there is vij wonders of the world. But because there are more wonderfull things then those which some have written of, I will sett downe such things as I thinck most wonderfull, and yet kepe the nomber of vij still.

1. The Bathes, at the citty of Bath, are accompted one, althowgh yet they are not so wonderfull, seing that the sulphur & brimston in the earth ys the cause therof; but this may pass well ynowgh for one.

2. The second some make to be the Stonehedge in Wiltshire, not farr from Salesbury. This monument was set vpp by Aurelius Ambrose, King of Brittains, about the yeare of our Lord 470, in remembrance of 460 barons & noblemen of the Brittains that were there slayne by treason of the Saxons, in the daies of Vortiger his predecessor, the picture of which stones are after to be seene in the description of Wiltshire.

3. There is at the Peak and other mountains in England, such hollow places vnder the ground, that many men have gone in & passed a good way, yet could they not come to the end therof. And being within have found so many rounes & places, that except they have a long lyne with them to follow, shall not hitt the way out agayne. Also within the said caves are found running rivers of waters, so deepe, that a man cannot with a long poale reach the bottome.

4. There are two rivers which put Suffolk from Norfolk that spring both out of one lake at Lophamford, the one is named Litle Ouse & ronneth westward, the other, named Waveney, ronneth estward towards Yermouth.

5. There is a well at Knaresborow in Yorkshire called the Dropping Well, which torneth into stone what soever is put or falleth into it, in the space of js or x monthes, and yet the thing shall kepe his proper forme & shape still, as I my self have seene a billet of wood, that so much as stood in the water, was very stone, the rest wood still.

6. The salt pitts in Cheshire, & one in Worcestershire, wherwith salt is made, may very well pass for a wonder, because they are allwaies found by a fresh river of water, and not nere the sea or any salt water.

7. The vjth & last may well be London Bridge, ffor that there is not the lyke in all the world agayne; and to make the nomber even, take Pawles Church in S London for the eight, whose lyke for greatnes is not † Christendome.

Hereafter ffolloweth the particuler description of every shyre in England, and beffore the same I have placed the armes of all them that have byn Erles of the same countrey. And first of Kent.

[he f. 13^b contains the Arms of the Earls of Kent — see Plate V.]

*KENT

Kent, called by the Romains Cantium, by the Brittains Caint, cometh first to hand to be spoken of, and lyeth sowth and sowthest next to France, where the narrow seas are but 24 myles broade. So that with a good wynd, a man may sayle in litle more then two howres from Dover to Callis, which is 30 myles. On the north syde it is devyded from Essex by the famous river of Thames, having the meane sea on the est, Sussex on the south, & Surrey on the west. This countrey contayneth in length est & west 50 myles, and in breadth north & south 25. Wherein are two citties namely Canterbury and Rochester, xvij market townes to say, Dover, Sandwich, Feuershim, Milton, Gravesend, Dartford, Sennock, Tunbridge, Malling, Wrotcham, Maidston, Cranbroke, Tenham, Ashford, Wye, Appledore, Rumney, & Hyde, and hath 398 parish churches. Of the scituation of all the said market townes somwhat shalbe said hereafter, and first of Canterbury & Rochester.

Canterbury (called in tymes past Durobreuis, and Durouernum, but now in Latin Cantuaria, & in Brittish Cancaint) was founded by Rudhudibras, about the yeare of the world 3078. Having in longitude 21 degrees 25 minutes, & in latitude 51 degrees 28 mi, and is scituate in a most pleasant place, distant from Douer, 12 myles, from Sandwich, 8, ffrom Feuersham, 6, & from Rochester, 20. Vppon the river of Stoure, which river coming from Ashford, passeth by Wye, Chilham, & Chartham, and having passed this cittie, goeth to Fordish, West Bere, Stadmarsh, and Stourmouth, where, not farr of, it devydeth it selffe into two parts, making (by this meanes) an Iland called Tenet. The lesser part ronning north, falleth into the sea betwixt Recolver & Gore End. The bigger part kepeth his course southest, aryveth at the fayre towne of Sandwich, & after torning northest, two myles of, falleth into the sea at the Cliffs End, and is called Sandwich Hauen. The cittie of Canterbury is a fayre & large citty, well walled, in compass round, having on the south syde the Castell, and on the north syde the goodly fayre Minster, or Cathedrall Church, called Christchurch, wherein are dyvers tombes & monuments of dyvers great princes, as, namely, King Henry the 4, Edward P of Wales, called the Black Prince, Thomas, Duke of Clarence, also of dyvers archbishopps & others.

[leaf 14

The River Stoure

[leaf 15a contains the plan of Canterbury see Plate XVIII]

Rochester ys but a litle cittie, but very ancient, as may appeare by the walles thereof, which now in many places are gone to decay. Also the Castell, which seemeth to be builded when the Tower of London was, and is lyke the same building. The cheiffest church is called St Andrewes. There is a very ffayre bridge of stone, ffounded by Sir Robt Knolles, Knight, with a chapell at the est end therof, which bridge is builded vppon pyles, lyke as London bridge is, I meane in the selffe same maner. The river of Medway passeth vnder the said bridge, which river springeth in Surrey, not farr from Starborow Castell, and passing by Edinbridge, cometh to Pensherst, where yt meeteth with another that cometh out of Sussex, and so keepe their course to Tunbridge, & from thence to Yalding, where (meeting with another river) yt becometh navigable, & passeth to Maidston, from thence to Rochester, where it is of such depth that all the Quenes Maiesties shipps do ryde there at a low water, all along the river, from Rochester to Vpnor Castell, and 6 myles thence, one part of the river falleth into the Thamise at Quinborow Castell, the other part, ronning estward towards Feuersham, maketh the famous Ile of Shepey, & the two litle ylandes called Elmsey & Harty, and then falleth into the sea at the Lands-end, and thus much touching ye cittie of Rochester, whose picture hereafter enseweth.

*[leaf 15/

The River Medway

[leaf 16a contains the plan of Rochester see Plate XIX]

Dover lyeth in a low valley vppon the sea syde, betwene two hilles, wherof one (that on the north side) hath a marvelous great & ancient castell, wherein are dyvers antiquities to be seene. The towne hath passing through it, a small brooke, which springeth 2 or 3 myles from thence. It is walled in some places, & hath iij churches, the cheiffest wherof is called Saint Martins, and was of late yeares a bishopprick.

*[leaf 16/

Sandwich standeth within two myles of the sea, nere the Cliffs end, vppon the river of Stoure, that cometh from Canterbury, and is a ffyne towne walled about, but inhabited most part with Netherlanders, where great store of bayes, and is also one of the Cincqports, as well as Douer, but Douer is the cheiffest.

Feuersham standeth westwards from Canterbury 6 myles, and about ij myles from the Ile of Harty (which is a prt of the Ile of Shepey). It hath two churches, wherof one of them hath the sepulcre of King Stephen, & Mauld his wyffe.

Mulleton, comonly called Milton, is hard by Sittingborne, distant from Feuersham 5 myles, & from Rochester 8.

Gravesend standeth vppon the Thamise, 5 myles from Rochester, & 6 from

*[leaf 17]

Dartford, where there is every tyde, a comon passage by water to London, which is 20 myles the which a man may pass, for *the* valew of two pence, in *the* comon barge & in a tiltbote for vjd

Dartford standeth within two myles of the Thamise, vppon the river of Darent, which cometh from Otford, 12 miles from London, & 6 from Gravesend

Sennock or *Senenoke* standeth within the mayne land, distant 5 litle myles from Otford, 5 from Tunbridge, and 7 from Malling

Tunbridge standeth vppon the river of Medway, 5 myles from Yalding, & as many from Sennock, and hath a litle prety countrey of *the* compass of 2 myles belonging to it, called The Territory of Tunbridge

Malling is 3 myles westward from Maidston, & as many north from Yalding

Wrotham is iij myles west from Malling

Maidston standeth vppon *the* river of Medway, 6 myles from Rochester, 5 from Lencham, & 4 from Yalding

Cranbroke standeth halff way betwixt Tunbridge & Rye, to say, 10 myles from the one, & xj from *the* other

Lencham standeth betwene Maidston & Wye, 6 myles from the one, & 7 from the other

Ashford standeth vppon the river of Stoure, yt passeth from thence to Wye, & so to Canterbury, distant from Wye 3 myles, from Lencham 7, and as many from Hyde

Hye standeth vppon the said river of Stoure, 3 myles from Ashford & 6 from Canterbury

Apledore standeth vppon *the* river of Rother, or Rotha, 4 myles from Rye, & 5 from Romney. Which river springeth in Sussex, at Argose Hill, & ronneth to Bewlham Ethingham Robartsbridge & Bedham Castell, where it devydeth Kent & Sussex till it come to Mattam fery, where it devydeth it self into two parts, making a round yland called Oxney, which belongeth to Kent. The bigger part therof, having visited Apledore, torneth south, & meeteth with his fellow agayne, and before the towne of Rye (receeving in certayne waters that come from Winchelsey), do discharge themselves into the sea, at *the* Camber Castell

Romney standeth vppon the sea syde, 6 myles from Rye, 5 from Apledore, 7 from Hyde, and is one of the port townes

Hyd, or *Hith* standeth vppon the sea syde, distant from Romney 7 myles, from Ashford 7, and from Dover 8, and is also one of the portes

ꝉ There remayneth yet iij things to be spoken of, before we depart out of Kent, and those are these —

The first is the great wood called Andreswald, but now, The Weld of Kent, which was in old tyme noted to begyn in Kent, and did contayne in length, est and west 120 myles & in breadth 30, so that it should appeare this wood did reach to *the* farthest part of Hamshire. Therfore it must needs be, that all *the* forrests & parks lying betwene these places were part of the same wood, namely those in Sussex & Ham-shire (wherof more shalbe sayd hereafter) and did but beginne in Kent. But besydes this, there are many goodly fayre parkes in Kent, as the Roiall manors & parks of Grenewich, Eltham, & Otford, besydes a nomber of others belonging to divers noble men, knights & gentlemen

ꝉ The other thing to be noted, is that Kent only now holdeth the old priveleges, which beffore the Conquest was holden throughout all England. For after the great battaill fought at Battell in Sussex, (by William Conqueror, Duke of Normandy; he repayred to the cittie of London, which was yelded to hym, and taking his jorney from thence to *the* castell of Dover, the Kentishmen being armed mett hym by the way, every man carrying a bowgh of a greene tree in their handes, and cominge nere the Duke sent embassadors to hym, to shew hym that they were come to meete hym as their leige lord, on condition that they might enjoy their antient liberties, otherwise they were redy to geve hym battaill

The Duke, perceyving how he was entrapped, did graunt them the same, which they enioy even at this day.

The third and last thing, is the sandes lying in the sea, called at this day Goodwin Sands, which in tymes past was mayne ground belonging to Goodwin, Erle of Kent, and was drowned by breaking in of the sea, in the yeare of our Lord 1097, and in the 15th yeare of K. William Rufus.

Castells in Kent *[leaf 19]

Canterbury	Milton	Deele	Ainsford
Rochester	Grauesend 2	Saltwood	Tong
Douer	Quinborow	Walmer	Layborn
Leedes	Cooling	Allington	Vpnor
Tunbridge	Sandowne	Shoram	

Manor Places belonging to the King

Greenewich	Otford	Douer Castell
Litham	Knoll	Dele Castell
Dartford	St Augustins	

[leaf 19b contains the Coat of Arms of Thomas Radcliff, Earl of Sussex see Plate XXII.]

SUSSEX

*Sussex taketh name of the Southsaxons, which was in tymes past a kingdome, *[leaf 20] contayning Sussex & Surrey, and had for their cheiff cittie Neomagum, now called Gilford. But because it is at this day devyded into two shyres or countries, therfore every countrie shalbe spoken of apart. This countrie of Sussex con- *Length &* tayneth in length, est & west, 60 myles, in breadth, but 16 or 18 at the most *breadth* broadest. It hath on the south syde the English Sea, on the west Hamshire, on the north Surrey, & on the northest Kent. Having Chichester at this day for *Market* the cheiff cittie, although some do accompt Lewis for the shyre towne. Besydes *townes* which cittie, it hath 18 market townes, namely, Rye, Winchelsey, Hasting, Brighthelmston, Pemsey, Shoram, Staning, Bramber, Brodwater, Tering, Arundell, Midherst, Petworth, Horsham, Est Grinsted, Lewis, Dichning & Hailsham. And *Parish* hath 312 parish churches. *Churches*

*Chichester, called in Brittish Cacicery, & (as it appeareth by some writers) *[leaf 20b] named Ceasers Chester by Julius Ceaser, who builded or repayred the same. It standeth in longitude, 19 degrees 22 minutes, & in latitude, 51 degrees 2 mi. Distant from Arundell 8 myles, from Midherst 7, from Hauant in Hamshire, 6, & from Portsmouth 10. in the very southwest corner of Sussex, & vppon a small river or brooke called Dell, which springeth 4 myles from thence, & having passed this cittie, about 3 myles beneath, falleth into the sea, making 2 Ilandes, called Thorney, & Halling, which last (being the greater) belongeth to Hamshire, and lyeth beffore Hauant, reaching within 3 myles of Portsmouth. The cittie it selff is not very great, but yet walled about & indifficent strong, having dyvers ffayre streets & lanes, but the cheiffest ornament therof is the Cathedrall Church.

Rye is a proper litle walled towne, standing vppon the mouth of the river Rother[1] (alredy described in Apuldor), distant from the said Apuldor 4 myles, from Winchelsey 2, and from Hasting 8, and is also one of the portes of the realme, and the cheiffest for passage betwixt England & France.

Winchelsey is also one of the port townes, & standeth wthin a myle of *[leaf 21] the sea, distant from Rye 2 myles, & from Hasting 6, and standeth after a strange maner in a low marish ground, and yet the towne it selff ys very high, having a

[1] 'Rother' in the MS

street going to the gate beginning low, & so goeth wynding, higher & higher, till it come to the towne gates

Hasting standeth vppon the sea syde, being also one of the portes of the realme, and is well walled about, distant from Winchelsey 6 myles, from Pemsey 8, and from Buttell 5

Pemsey standeth within two myles the sea, vppon 2 small brookes which meet there, and having passed the towne a myle of, do meet with another river, & so fall into the sea, being there called Pemsey Hauen

Brighthelmsted (comonly called Brighthemston) standeth vppon the sea syde, distant from Shoram 4 myles, and from Lewiss almost 6

New Shoram standeth vppon the mouth of a small river which cometh from Bramber, distant from Old Shoram one myle, from Bramber 3, from Brodwater 3½, from Terring 4, and from Brighthemston 4

Staning standeth within a myle of Bramber, 4 myles from New Shoram, & 3 from Brodwater

[fo. 121ᵇ.]

Bramber standeth betwene Staning & Shoram a myle from the one, & 3 from the other, vppon the same river that ronneth to Shoram

Brodwater standeth a myle from the sea, but it hath no water coming to it, distant from 3½ myles from Shoram, & vij from Arundell

Terring standeth lyke Brodwater a myle from thence, & a myle from the sea, having also no water coming to it, & is 6 myles from Arundell

Arundell is a proper towne, with a castell, which geveth name to the ancient howse of the Erles of Arundell, and standeth vppon the river Arun, distant from the meane sea 3 myles, from Brodwater 7, from Terring 6, from Staning 9, from Petworth 8 & from Chichester 8

Midherst standeth vppon a branch of the said river of Arun, which springeth not far from Petersfeld, in Hamshire, distant 8 myles from Chichester north, 7 est from Petersfeld & 5 west from Petworth

Petworth standeth 5 myles est from Midherst, 8 from Arundell, & 12 from Horsham

[fo. 22.]

Horsham standeth on the north syde of Sussex within 3 myles of Surrey, distant from Rigate, in Surrey, 9 myles, & from Est Grinsted 9, vppon a litle brooke which springeth in St Leonards Forrest therby, and meeting with the Arun, which cometh from Midherst, passeth to Arundell, & so into the sea, being there called Arundell Hauen

Est Grensted (so called for diffrence of West Grensted), standeth also within¹ a myles of Surrey, & within¹ 4 of Kent but hath no water coming to it, and is distant 9 myles from Horsham, & as many from Rigate, in Surrey, ffor these 3 townes Rigate, Horsham, & Est Grinsted, do stand in triangle 9 myles one from the other

Dichning standeth lower towards the Downes, 5 myles from Lewiss, & as many from Brighthemston, for these 3 townes stand also in triangle. It hath no water coming to it

Lewiss (next to Chichester) is the cheiffest towne in Sussex, and the place where the Sessions & Assises are kept, so that some do accompt it the shyre towne, and standeth within 5 myles of the meane sea, vppon a river, which springeth not far from Horsham, & kepeth his course estwards, southest, & lastly south & (having receaved in divers other rivers) passeth this towne, and 5 myles thence falleth into the sea, making a Hauen called New Hauen

[fo. 22.]

Hailsham is a dry towne lying 3 myles north from Pemsey, and 9 est from Lewiss

There lyeth on the north syde of Sussex 4 great fforrests palled about & within 2 myles one of the other containing in length est & west, nere 20 myles (accompting the ground betwene them which is 6 myles), whereof a word or two, and so an end of Sussex

¹ "with" in the MS.

The first forrest lying toward the est, is Waterdown Forrest, which is 5 myles long, north & south, the north end of yt partcth Kent from Sussex, and is 3 myles brode, wherein standeth my L. of Abergucnies place, named Eredge

The second is Ashdowne Forrest, which is square, 4 myles every way. In the northest corner wherof is Buckherst, the manor place belonging to the L. Buckherst

The third is Word Forrest, which is 4 myles long & 3 brode, 1½ myle distant from Est Grinsted

The fourth & last is St Leonards Forrest, not farr from Horsham, which is in length north & south, 7 myles, & in breadth 3

As Sussex and Surrey was in tymes past one countrey, so did the Erles threof vse both names in their stile, but since they have byn seperated, the Erles of Surrey have retayned the ancient armes therof, as appeareth on the other syde

[leaf 23r contains Coats of Arms of Earls of Surrey see Plate VI]

SURREY

Surrey, the other part of *the* South-Saxon kingdome, did first take name (as *[leaf 23v]* we may well conjecture) of Suthrie, which in the Saxon speech is as much to say as South kingdome, for so likewise Kent was by them called Cantric This countrey of Surrey contayneth in length, est & west, 26 myles, & in breadth *Length and* 20, being almost 4 square. On the north syde it is devided from Midlesex & *breadth* a corner of Buckinghamshire by the river of Thamise, having Barkshire on *the* west, Hamshire on the southwest, Sussex on the south, & Kent on the est. The cheiffest towne in Surrey I accompt Southwark, although the Sessions and Shyre daies are comonly kept at Gilford. Besydes Southwark, it hath 6 market townes, *Market* to say, Gulford, Farnham, Godalming, Kingston, Rigate, & Croidon, of which *Townes* townes, Southwark, Gilford, & Rigate, have Burgeses in the Parlement House, and 2 borowes more, to say, Blechinglegh and Gatton, but these 2 are no market townes, except they have byn made of late. Surrey hath in it the two Roiall *Parish* manors of Richmond & Otcland, and hath 140 parish churches *Churches*

Southwark, although it be part of London, and one of the 26 wardes therof, *[leaf 24]* yet it standeth in Surrey, having in it the prison called The Whyte Lion, which prison serveth for the county of Surrey. All this borow of Southwark was purchased by the Cittie of London, in the tyme of K. Edward the vj, so that it is all now within the Liberties of London, and hath in it 5 great parish churches, to say, St Mary Overs, St Olaffs, St Thomas, St George, & St Saviors

Guilford was in tyme past, the cheiffest towne both of Sussex & Surrey, and was called, as some do think, by the Romains, Neomagus, or Neomagun. The castell being marvelous old, and the 3 churches in the towne, declare it to be of great antiquity. This towne standeth distant from Farnham 7 myles, from Rigate 12, & 25 from London; vppon a river which some call Wey, which *The river of* springeth at Aulton, in Hamshire, & kepeth his course estwards to Farnham, *Wey* Godalming, and then torning northwards, cometh to this towne, & 10 myles from thence falleth into the Thamise, nere vnto Otcland

Farnham standeth on the west end of Surrey, within a myle of Hamshire, *[leaf 24v]* vppon the river of Wey, as beffore is said, distant from Aulton, in Hamshire, 6 myles, & from Gilford 7

Godallming standeth vppon the said river of Wey, 3 myles from Gilford, & 4 from Farnham

Kingston standeth vppon the Thamise, 10 myles from London, 6 from Croidon, from Otcland 5 miles, & from Rcchmond 3, xx from Gilford, & one from Hampton Court, in Midlesex. In this towne (beffore the Conquest) were the Kings of England crowned, vppon high skaffolds, that they might be seene of the people

Rigate is distant from Croidon 7 myles, from Horsham & Est Grinsted, in Sussex, 9 myles. It hath no water coming to it.

Croidon standeth halff way betwixt London & Rigate, 7 myles from ech. There passeth from it a small brook, which falleth into the Thamise at Wansworth, 5 myles west from London. *Foure myles from Croidon, & iij litle on's from Kingston, is the princely howse of Nonsuch which belongeth to the Erle of Arundell.

There passeth throwgh the middest of Surrey a river (which some call Moule), that springeth in Word Forrest, in Sussex, and cometh within two myles of Rigate, where it passeth vnder the ground almost 3 myles, and afterwards cometh forth agayne, & kepeth his course to Stoke & Coucham, and 4 myles thence falleth into the Thamise, nere Hampton Court.

[leaf 25*b* contains Coats of Arms of the Earls of Southampton — see Plate VII.]

HAMSHIRE

Hamshire taketh name of *the* shyre towne of Hampton, comonly called Southampton, ffor diffrence of Northampton. This countrey contayneth in length from Portsmouth, in the south to Statfeldsay in *the* north, 34 myles, and in breadth 20, and in some places 25 myles, having Dorcetshire on *the* southwest, Wiltshire on the west, Barkshire on *the* north Surrey & Sussex on the est, and the Ile of Wight on the south, which iland belongeth vnto this shyre, as also dyvers others, as Jersey, Garnsey, & others, which lye vppon *the* coast of France, as hereafter shalbe declared. In which countrie (besydes the cittie of Winchester), there is 18 market townes, namely, Southampton, Portsmouth, Faram, Suthwik, Hauant, Bishoppswaltham Petersfeld Alresford Aulton, Odiam, Basingstoke, Kingsclere, Andouer Stockbridge, Rumsey, Ringwood, Lemington and Christs-church, and hath of other townes & villages to *the* nomber of 248, which market townes shalbe spoken of in order, after I have done with Winchester, which cittie as it is very antient and a Bishopps seat, so doth the said Bishopprick in revenews pass all other bishopprieks in England.

[leaf 26*b* contains Coats of Arms of Earls of Winchester — see Plate VIII.]

*[View of Winchester at the top — see Plate XX.]

Winchester called by *the* Brittans Caerwint, by *the* Romains Venta, (in whose tyme it was cheiff cittie of *the* Simeney, which now are the people of Hamshire,) is now called in Latin Wintonia & Vinton, and was founded (as some hold opinion) by Rud Hudibras, King of Brittains, who budded Canterbury also. It standeth almost in the middest of Hamshire, vppon a small river, which some call Itchin, that runneth from thence to Southampton, and is distant from Southampton 10 myles, from Rumsey 7, and from Stockbridge 6. It is an ancient cittie, fayre, large & well walled, and was in tymes past cheiff cittie of the West Saxon kingdome, as also before that the place where King Arthur did comonly kepe his Court as in the Castell, which is very ancient there hangeth the Round Table, which I have seene & is kept there for an ancient monument, also in the Cathedrall Church of *the* cittie are dyvers monuments of kings that were beffore the Conquest and of Cardinall Henry Beauford, with dyvers other Bishopps of the same cittie.

*[Arms of Southampton at the top — see Plate I.]

Southampton, called in Brittish, Hrs Antoms, is *the* towne which geveth name to the whole shyre, as afforsaid and standeth vppon a gulf of *the* sea, which is 6 myles long & 2 brode, reaching from Calshot Castell vpp to Southampton from which Castell is 4 myles to *the* Ile of Wight. Some wryte that it tooke name of one Hamon, that Arinragus, K. of Brittains, did there throw into the sea, and is distant from Portsmouth xj myles, from Winchester 10, & from Rumsey 5. It is an ancient towne, walled, and well traded with marchandize, & hath (as I heare say) 7 parish churches

*Portsmouth standeth on the sea syde, in the Iland called Portsey, distant from Faram, Suthwik & Hauant, lyke distance of 5 myles, and is but a litle towne diched about, with 2 ffayre castells, which are the strength therof It tooke name of a Saxon named Port, who landed there with his 2 sonnes, about the yeare of our Lord 471. Within the gulf or haven of Portsmouth, 3 myles thence, at the foote of the Downes called Portsdowne, standeth the ancient towne & castell of Portchester, called by the Brittains Caerperis, which now is gone to decay *[leaf 28]

Faram standeth vppon a small river which cometh from Suthwik, & ffalleth into the gulff at Portchester, & is 2 myles from Portchester, & 2 from Suthwik

Suthwik standeth vppon the said brooke, 2 myles from Faram, on the other syde of the Downes

Hauant standeth vppon a gulf of the sea, having an iland called Haling on the south, a mile distance, & is 6 myles west from Chichester & 4 ffrom Portsmouth

Bishoppswaltham standeth in the forrest syde, called Waltham Forrest, 6 myles from Faram & Suthwik, 7 from Winchester, & from Southampton 8

*Petersfild lyeth on the est syde of Hamshire, within a myle or a litle more of Sussex, 9 myles north from Hauant, & as many south from Aulton, not farr from a small river called Arun, which ronneth to Arundell in Sussex *[leaf 28v]

Alresford standeth betwene Winchester & Aulton, 6 myles from the one, & 8 from the other

Aulton standeth vppon the head of the river Wey, yt passeth from thence to Farnham, & so to Gilford, distant from Farnham 6 myles, & from Odiam 5

Odiam is 5 myles from Aulton, & as many ffrom Basingstoke

Basingstoke is 4½ myles from Odiam & 7 ffrom Kingsclere, & within a myle of the princely place called Basinghowse, which belongeth to the Marques of Winchester

Kingsclere lyeth on the north end of Hamshire, 5 myles from Newbery, in Barkshire, & from Andouer 10

Andouer standeth on the west syde of Hamshire, vppon a litle broke, which ronneth from thence to Stockbridge, 5 myles from Lurgishall, in Wiltshire

Stockbridge standeth vppon the river of Stoke, yt springeth within 2 myles of Basingstoke, at Church Stokeley, & ronneth westwards to Overton & Whitchurch where *it torneth southwest to Stockbridge, & afterwards south to Rumsey, & falleth into the gulf at Southampton, this towne is distant from Salesbury xj myles, & from Winchester 6 *[leaf 29]

Rumsey standeth vppon the said river distant from Winchester & Stockbridge 7 myles, & from Southampton 6

Ringwood standeth within 2 myles of Dorcetshire, on the west syde of the New Forrest, in Hamshire, & vpon the est syde of the river of Avon which cometh from Salesbury, distant from Christchurch 6 myles, & from Cranborne, in Dorcetshire, 5 myles

Christchurch standeth vppon the river of Stoure, which cometh[1] out of Dorcetshire, and at this towne meeteth with the river of Avon, & so 2 myles hence do fall into the sea, maketh a haven called Christchurch Haven. This towne is 9 myles from Lemington & 6 from Ringwood

Lemington standeth on the sea syde, halff way betwixt Christchurch & Southampton, 9 litle myles from the one, & 9 great from the other, vppon the mouth of a small river that cometh out of the New Forrest & here falleth into the sea

*Forrests in Hamshire *[leaf 29v]

1 The New Forrest (lying on the southwest corner of Hamshire) doth

[1] The words "cometh out" are repeated in the MS

contayne in length 12 myles, & in breadth 8 myles. John Harding wryteth that K. William Rufus (to make the same forrest) did overthrow 4 abbaies & 17 parish churches, besydes which forrest there are dyvers others in Hamshire, whose names do follow.

 2 Buckholt Forrest lyeth uppon Wiltshire, nere unto Stockbridge.
 3 Westbere Forrest is hard by Winchester.
 4 Estbere Forrest lyeth by Suthwik.
 5 Waltham Forrest by Bishoppswaltham, being parted by a river from Estbere Forrest.
 6 Wulmer Forrest, betwene Petersfeld & Farnham.
 7 Alesholt Forrest, betwene Aulton & Farnham.
 8 Pamber Forrest lyeth on the north end of Hamshire, nere Barkshire, not far from Kingsclere.
 9 Chutchamshire Forrest lyeth most part in Hamshire, the rest in Wiltshire, and is hard by Andouer, taking name of Chute, in Wiltshire.

BARKSHIRE

[Hed. 50] 'Anno Dñi 871. In the daies of King Etheldred we read of one Ethelwold, Duke of Barcoke (now called Bukshire), who was slayne by the Danes. Since which tyme I know not of any Duke or Erle that hath borne name of the said countrey.

[f. 59] 'Next to Hamshire, on the north, are those people which were called by the Romans Atrabates, now Barkshiremen, which countrey (as Fabian & others do wryte) did first take name of a bare oke standing in the forrest of Windsor, under which the men of the shyre did meete together,[1] wherby it was then called Bareokeshire, and now short Barkshire. To which opinion I rather yeld (seing the name of Barcoke is found in ancient wryters) then to those that thinck it to be called Bergshire, that is to say, the hilly shyre, because berg in Saxon is a hill, and I know no cause why it should not take name of the towne of Barkam, not far from Okingham. This countrey is in length, est & west, 40 myles, in breadth, in some places, 22 myles, in other some 16, 12, & in one place but 4 myles, which is about Reading, and is fashioned much lyke the sole of a mans left foote. It is separated on the north syde from Oxfordshire & Buckinghamshire by the river of Thamise, which (because it ronneth so crooked) maketh the shyre to be so narrow in some places, & broad in other some. It hath on the est end Surrey, on the south syde Hamshire, & on the west end Wiltshire. Wherein are xii market townes, & 139 parish churches.

[f. 59 b.] 'Reding, called by the Romans Pontium (as most men hold opinion), standeth where the river of Kenet falleth into the Thamise, distant from Henley 5 myles, & 12 myles from Windsor, which river of Kennet springeth in Wiltshire, & passeth from Marlborow to Ramsbury, Hungerford, Newbery, & so to Reding. Reding Abbay was founded by K. H. 1, who was there buried.

 Wallingford was in tymes past cheiffe cittie of all this countrey, anciently named Calena, and standeth uppon the Thamise, 6 myles from Abington & 9 from Oxford. There is yet (as I heare say) iij churches in the towne, which is gone much to decay, especially the Castell, which was builded by Ranulf, Erle of Chester who was Baron therof.

 Abington standeth where the small river of Ock falleth into the Thamise, 4 litle myles from Oxford.

 Faringdon standeth within 2 myles of the Ise, or Thamise, 4 myles from Lechlade, in Glocestershire, & as many from Heworth, in Wiltshire.

 Wantage standeth in the Vale of Whytehorse, 6 myles from Abington, & as many from Lamborne, uppon a small river, which iij myles of, ffalleth into the Ock, and so ronneth to Abington.

 [1] "togeather" in the MS.

Lamborne standeth on the west end of Barkshire, distant from Ramsbury, in Wiltshire, 5 myles, & 6 from Hungerford

Hungerford standeth vppon the river of Kennet, in the west end of Barkshire 6 myles from Lamborne, & 7 from Newbery

Est Hsly standeth in the middest of Barkshire, 7 myles south from Wallingford, & as many north from Newbery, a myle from West Ilsley

Newbery standeth vppon the river of Kennet, 15 myles from Reding, and is a great & fayre towne, having water ronning through the streets therof, lyke as at Salesbury

Okingham is 5 myles from Reding & 8 from Windsor. The church of this towne standeth in Wiltshire, & yet Wiltshire is not nye it by 24 myles (except 2 litle peeces therof, which ly by Statfeldsey, 4 myles from this towne)

Maidenhead standeth vppon the Thamise, 10 myles from Reding & 5 from Windsor

Windsor standeth vppon the Thamise, on the est end of Barkshire, 20 myles from London, and is the only bewty of Barkshire, as also one of the most renowmed & famous places of England, by reason of the Castell, whose lyke is hardly to be found in any other countrey. In the church of the said Castell is the sepulture of certaine kings, and is the place where the honorable order of St George (intituled the Garter) was first established & yearly holden

[leaf 32r contains Coats of Arms of the Earls of Wiltshire see Plate IX]

WILTSHIRE

Wiltshire taketh name of Wilton, which in old tyme was the head towne of the shyre, having in it 12 parish churches. But now Salesbury (which is 2 myles thence) hath taken away the glory therof. Others affirme that it taketh name of the River Willug, because in some old copies it is written Willug-shire, & now short Wiltshire. The people of this countrey were called by the Romans Seunani or their cheiff cittie Seucrus, now Salesbury. This countrey of Wiltshire contayneth in length, north and south, 40 myles, & in breadth about 26. Having Somersetshire on the west, Gloucestershire on the north, Barkshire & Hamshire on the est, & Dorcetshire on the south. In which countrey (besydes the cittie of Salesbury) there are 15 other townes, which have voices in the Parliament, namely, Creklade, Marlborow, Lungshall, Duncton, Hindon, Westbury, Malmsbury, Wotton Basset, Old Salesbury, Wilton, Hetesbury, Deuyses, Chippenham, Calne, & Great Bedwin. To these may be added 9 more, which are also market townes, as Castlecomb, Trubridge, Mere, Bradford, Est Lauington, Warmister, Amsbury, Ramsbury, & Hiworth, and hath in it about 276 parish churches

[leaf 33r contains Coats of Arms of the Earls of Salisbury see Plate X]

*[Plan of Salisbury, 1588, at the top see Plate XXI]

Salsbury or *Sarisbury*, called in Latin, Sarum, and in British, Caer Seuerus & Caer Caredoc, standeth in the southest corner of Wiltshire vppon the river of Auon, distant from Amesbury 6 myles, from Duncton 4 myles, & within 6 myles of Hamshire. It is a fayre & large citty, having fresh water ronning through every streete. In the Cathedrall Church of our Lady are dyvers sepultures of the Erles of Salesbury & of Bishopps of that Sea. The said river of Auon springeth in Sauernak Forrest, & passeth southwards by Wotton Milton Pewsey Maningford, Newenton, Vphaven, Cheselbury Nether Hauen Milston Durrington Amesbury Great Deinford, Litle Deinford, Old Salesbury & so to this New Salesbury, where it taketh in the Willug on the west which cometh from Wilton, & another on the est, and so passeth to Duncton, & from thence entring into Hamshire cometh to Ringwood, Auon & Sopley, & at[1] Christ Church meeteth with the Stoure, that cometh out of Dorcetshire, & so falleth into the sea.

*Old Salisbury is 2 myles north from New Salesbury

Wilton is 2 myles west from Salesbury, by whose ruines a man may yet well perceaue what it hath byn in tymes past. Hard by the towne is a stately house or pallace belonging to the Erle of Penbroke

Dunton standeth vppon the Auon, 4 myles beneath Salesbury, & within 2 myles of Hamshire

Mere standeth in the southwest corner of Wiltshire, within a myle of Dorcetshire, 5 myles west from Hindon

Hindon is about 14 myles west from Salesbury & 6 northest from Shaftesbury, in Dorcetshire

Warminster standeth 7 myles north northest from Mere, vppon one of the heads of the River Willug, 5 myles from Frome, in Somersetshire

Westbury is 3 myles north from Warmester, and within 3 myles of Somersetshire. It is comonly called Westbury vnder the Playne, because it is hard by the Playne of Salesbury

Est Lauington lyeth also vnder the Playne of Salesbury, about 7 or 8 myles estward of Westbury, & fyve from the Deuises

The Deuises is a market towne with a Castell, standing in the middest of Wiltshire, distant north ffrom Est Lauington 5 myles, and south from Calne 6 myles

*Trubridge is 4 myles northward from Westbury, & 2 southest from Bradford

Bradford standeth vppon the riuer of Auon within litle more then a myle of Somersetshire, distant from Bath 5 myles, & from Phillipps Norton 4

Castlecomb standeth on the west syde of Wiltshire within 2 myles of Glocestershire, 4 myles from Chippenham, & as many from Marsfeld, in Glocestershire

Chippenham or Chipnam standeth vppon the river of Auon, aforenamed, 4 myles from Castlecomb, & in London way

Calne is 4 myles est from Chippenham, & in London way also, from Bristow

Malmesbury standeth on the head of the said river of Auon, in the northwest corner of Wiltshire within 2 myles of Glocestershire 7 myles from Castlecomb, & 7 from Wotton Basset. K. Athelston was here buried An° 940

Wotton-Basset standeth betwene Malmsbury & Marlborow, 7 myles from the one, & 8 from the other

Crekelade standeth on the head of the Thamise, on the north end of Wiltshire, 5 myles from Wotton Basset, & as many from Hiworth

Hiworth standeth on a hill, on the northest corner of Wiltshire, within litle more then a myle of Barkshire

*Marlborow, a ffayre market towne (with the oldest castell that ever I sawe), standeth vppon the small river of Kennet, 4 myles from Ramsbury, & 5 from Bedwin

Ramsbury standeth on the said river, 4 myles ffrom Hungerford, in Barkshire, but whether it be a market towne or no I know not

Gret Bedwin is 4 myles south from Hungerford, & 6 from Lurgishall

Lurgishall standeth on the est syde of Wiltshire, by Chute Forrest, within a myle of Hamshire

Ambresbury or Imbersbury (comonly called Amesbury) standeth vppon the river of Auon, 6 myles north from Salesbury

Forrests in Wiltshire

Bradon Forrest, by Wotton Basset
Aldborne Chase, by Ramsbury
Pewsham Forrest, by Chippenham
Blackmore Forrest, by Pewsham Forrest
Sauernak Forrest, by Marlborow

[1] In the MS "not far from" is scratched through, and "at" inserted

Chute Forrest, the halff wherof lyeth in Hamshire, as beffore in Hamshire hath byn declared

*Two myles west from Ambrose-bury, vppon Salesbury Playne, is the Stonhedge, *[leaf 35b] one of the 7 wonders of England, sett vpp by Aurelius Ambrose, K of Brittains, about the yeare of our Lord 470, as in the beginning of this booke hath byn declared, the Picture of which I have here placed

[The remainder of the page is occupied with a view of Stonehenge see Plate XXII]

*[Coats of Arms of Marquises of Dorset at the top see Plate XI]   *[leaf 36]

DORCETSHIRE

Dorcetshire lyeth on the sea syde, reaching from Hamshire to Deuonshire, which is in length, est & west, 40 myles, the breadth, from Gillingham Forrest in the north, to the sea, is about 24 myles, but this is in the middest, for at ech end it is much narrower, because it is in proportion losengewise On the north syde it joyneth vppon Somersetshire & Wiltshire In which countrey there is 21 market townes, namely, Dorchester, Frampton, Burport, Lyme, Bemister, Eversholt, Cerne Sherborn, Shaftesbury, Sturmister, Blandford, Wimborne, Cranborne, Wirtwood, Poole, Corf, Wareham, Midleton, Bere, Waymouth, & Buton, and hath about 279 parish churches

*Dorchester is the towne which geveth name to all the whole countrey, and *[leaf 36b] standeth on the south syde of the shyre, vppon the river of Frame or Frome, distant 4 myles from the sea, which river, not far from Wareham, falleth into the gulf at Poole

Frampton standeth vppon the same river of Frame, 3 myles westward from Dorchester

Burport is 8 myles westward from Frampton, & within litle more then a myle of the sea

Lyme is a ffyne towne standing on the sea syde, within a myle of Deuonshire, 6 myles west from Burport

*Bemister is 4 myles directly north from Burport, vppon a small river which *[leaf 37] some call Bier, that ronneth from thence to Burport, & not far from thence falleth into the sea

Evershott is 5 myles northest from Bemister, & 7 from Sherborne

Cerne is 4 myles northward from Dorchester, & iij from Frampton, where in tymes past hath by an Abbay

Sherborne standeth on the northwest syde of the shyre, within a myle of Somersetshire, in the way from the west countrey to London, distant from Evill, in Somersetshire, 4 myles, from Sturmister 6, and from Shaftesbury 10 King Ethelbert is buried at Sherborne who died in An° 867

Shaftsbury standeth on a hyll on the northest corner of the shyre, within a myle of Wiltshire, & in the way also from Excester to London This towne was in tymes past a Bishopprick, from whence it was translated to Salesbury

Sturmister standeth on the river of Stoure which springeth in Wiltshire, at Sturton (a manor place belonging to the L Sturton), and entring into Dorcetshire, passeth by Gillingham through Gillingham Forrest, receiving divers rivers by the way, cometh to Sturmister, & from thence to Blandford, Wimborne, & lastly to Christschurch, in Hamshire, where it meeteth with the Auon, which cometh from Salesbury, & not farr of falleth into the sea This towne is 6 myles from Sherborne, & 5 from Shaftesbury

*Blandford standeth on the said river of Stoure 5 myles southest from Sturmister *[leaf 37b]

Wimborne standeth on the said river, 6 myles southest from Blandford, and 3 north from Poole It is comonly called Wimborne Minster, where dyvers princes & noblemen are buried, as K Etheldred, An° 872, John Beauford, Duke of Somerset & Marques Dorcet, with others

3

Cranborne standeth on the est end of Dorcetshire, within 2 myles of Wiltshire, & within 3 of Hamshire, distant north from Wimborn 7 myles

Hurtweed is 4 myles south from Cranborne, but whether it be a market towne or no, I know not

Poole standeth in a litle Peninsula within a great gulf of the sea 4 myles directly south from Wimborne, & iij from the meane sea, and is one of the best townes in all the shyre

Corf Castle & towne standeth in the middest of the Ile of Purbeck although it be no iland, but a peninsula, being 6 myles broad & 10 myles long. It is 2 myles from the Gulf of Poole & 3 from the sea

Wareham standeth betwene 2 rivers the Frame & the Piddle, which within a myle est therof do fall into the Gult of Poole, & is distant from Poole 5 myles, & from Corf 4

Bere standeth more into the land, 5 myles northwest from Wareham

Middleton standeth in the very middest of Dorcetshire, 4 myles northwest from Bere, & 7 northest from Dorchester

Waymouth and *Kingsincombe* do stand one against the other on the mouth of a litle river which there falleth into the sea 5 myles south from Dorchester, & 3 from Portland Castell

Burton standeth on the sea syde, 2 myles from Burport, but whether it be a market towne or no, I know not

The Ile of Portland lyeth on the south syde of this shyre in the sea. It is 2 myles long north & south, & the breadth is a myle & a halff. To the which at a low water a man may go on foote by a cawsey of sand, or gravell

Forrests in Dorcetshire

Gillingham Forrest on the north
Holt Forrest on the est end

Vales

The Vale of Whitehart alias Blakemore, betwene Sherborne & Eversholt
The Vale of Marshwood, on the west end of the shyre

[leaf 38b contains Coats of Arms of Dukes of Somerset — see Plate XII Nos 1 to 4]

SOMERSETSHIRE

Somersetshire hathe the Severne Sea on the northwest, Glocestershire on the north, Wiltshire on the est, Dorcetshire on the south, and Devonshire on the southwest. The length therof est & west 50 myles, the breadth in the middest is 27 myles, an[d] on the est end it is 30 myles broade, but towards the west yt groweth narrower & narrower, so that at the very west end it is but 8 myles broade. In which countrey (besydes the citties of Bath & Welles, & a peece of Bristow) there is 30 other market townes, the which I will name in order as they lye amongst which townes there is one called Somerton of which (as I thinck) the whole countrey taketh name, and hath about 476 parish churches

[The remainder of the page is occupied with Coats of Arms of the Earls of Bath — see Plate XIII]

*[View of Bath at the top — see Plate XXI]

Bath lyeth on the northest corner of Somersetshire, compassed almost round about with the river of Avon, distant southest from Bristow 10 myles, & southwest from Marsfeld in Glocestershire, 5 myles. It is but a litle cittie, yet one of the most ancientest in England, whereunto Welles is added, & so do both make one Bishopprick

Kensham or Carnsham standeth on the south syde of the said river of Avon, 4 myles from Bristow, & 6 from Bath

Pensford standeth 4 myles southward from Kensham, on a small brook called Chute, which, at Kensham falleth into the Avon.

Phillipps-Norton is 4 myles southward from Bath.

Froum-Selwood is 4 myles southward of Phillipps Norton, and on the north end of Selwood Forrest.

Shepton-Mallet is 6 myles southwest froum Selwood, & 4 from Glassenbury.

Welles standeth at the foote, on the south syde of Mendipp Hills, 3 myles northwest from Shepton Mallet, & 4 myles north from Glassenbury. It hath the name of Wells, because of dyvers well springs that are therein. It is walled, & is a cittie, making with Bath one Bishopprick.

Axbridge is 7 myles northwest from Welles, & not farre from a river named Ax, which springeth at Wokeyhole, hard by Welles, and within a myle estward of this towne is Chedder Rock, out of which springeth a broke of water in such abundance that it dryveth 12 milles within a quarter of a myle of his head.

Bruton standeth on the head of a small river called Brier, & at the south end of Selwood Forrest, 5 myles southest from Shepton Mallet.

Glassenbury standeth in the Ile of Aueland, which is no iland, but enclosed *leaving?* betwene 2 rivers, called Brier & Solway. This was in tymes past a famous place, because of the Abbay there, where dyvers kings of the realme have byn buried, as K. Arthur, K. Edmund I, An° 946, K. Edgar, An° 975, K. Edmund Ironside, An° 1017, and hard by, on a high hill, is the Tor, called Glassenbury Torr.

Wine-Caunton is 3 myles southest from Bruton, & within 2 myles of Dorcetshire.

Quene-Camell is 6 myles southest from Wine Caunton, and standeth on a small brook, which two myles thence, or litle more falleth into the Ivell.

Ivell standeth on the head of the river of Ivell, which there parteth Somersetshire from Dorcetshire, 4 myles west from Sherborne, & in the way to London.

Ilchester or *Ivelchester* standeth uppon the said river of Ivell, 4 myles from Ivell, & as much more from Quene Camell.

Somerton is 3 myles north northwest from Ichester, uppon a small river named Care, which 7 myles west from thence falleth into the said Ivell.

Langport standeth uppon the¹ afforsaid river of Ivell, 4 myles southwest from Somerton, & 6 from Ilchester.

Martock standeth in the Isle of Muchney, which is no iland, but enclosed betwene 2 rivers the Ivell & the Parret, 3 myles from Langport, & 4 from Ilchester.

Pedderton (comonly called *South Pedderton*) standeth on the other syde of *left?* the river Parret, within 2 myles of Martock.

Crookhorne standeth on the head of the river of Parret, 4 myles south from Pedderton, & within litle more then a myle of Dorcetshire, in the way to London.

Chard standeth also on the south syde of Somersetshyre, in the way to London, within halff a myle of Dorcetshire, 6 myles west from Crookhorne.

Ilminster is 3 myles northward from Chard, & 4 westward from South Pedderton, not farr from the river of Ill.

Bridgewater standeth on the west syde of the river of Ivell, 10 myles west from Glassenbury. This river of Ivell is the principallest river in all Somersetshire, and springeth not farr from Sherborn in Dorcetshire, and so passeth to Ivell, Ilchester, & not farr from Langport taketh in the Parret & the Ill and 4 myles lower the Tone which cometh from Taunton, and 2 myles from thence the Care which cometh from Somerton, and arriveth lastly at Bridgewater & 6 myles north from thence falleth into the Seaverne Sea, taking in certayne small brookes on the west syde.

Huntspill standeth in Brentmarsh, betwene 2 rivers, the Ivell & the Brier 4 myles north of Bridgewater, & within two myles of the sea.

¹ erasure in MS.

*_Taunton_ is a brave great towne, standing in a very frutefull soyle, vppon the river of Tone, which 6 myles falleth into the Ivell, and is distant from Bridgewater southwest 7 myles & as much northwest from Ilmister

Bishopps-Lidiard is 5½ myles northwest from Taunton, on a small broke, which 3 myles thence falleth into the Tone

Milverton is 3 myles southwest from Bishopps Lediard, vppon a small brook, which also falleth into the Tone

Wellington standeth vppon the said river of Tone, 2½ myles south from Milverton, & 5 from Taunton

Winchscomb is 2 myles northwest from Milverton, & not farr from the head of the said river of Tone

Dulverton (which some call _Damerton_) standeth within a litle more then a myle of Devonshire, & on a small river, which not farr of, falleth into the Ex, which runneth through Devonshire to Excester

Watchet standeth on the sea syde, 10 myles westward from Bridgewater

Dunster standeth also by the sea syde, 4 myles directly west from Watchet

Minhead standeth also vppon the sea syde, 2 myles from Dunster, from this towne is a comon passage over the Seavern Sea, to Silly, in Glamorganshire, which is 17 myles

*_Forrests in Somersetshyre_

Selwood Forrest, on the est end
Nerach Forrest, on the south, by Ilmister

Mores

Gedney More, by Welles
Sege More, betwene Welles & Glassenbury
Sedege More, southwest of Glassenbury
Heth More, betwene Glassenbury & Brentmarsh
Audrey More, hard by Sedege More
Quenes More, not farr from Bridgewater
North More, on the west syde of the river Ivell
Ex More, in the very west end of Somersetshire, where the river of Ex springeth

*[Coats of Arms of Erls of Devonshire at top — see Plate XI.]

DEVONSHIRE

Devonshire is one of the greatest shyres in England. It hath on the north end the Seavern Sea, on the south end the English Sea, on the west syde Cornwall, & on the est Somersetshire, & a peece of Dorsetshire. The length from the north to the south is 58 myles, the breadth in the middest & at the south end is 50 myles, but on the north end it is but 30. In which countrey (besydes the cittie of Excester) there is 36 market townes, and about 456 parish churches, besides villages, gentlemens howses, & castells whereof there is no small nomber

[If of 43 contains Coats of Arms of Dukes of Exeter, and of the city of Exeter — see Plates XIII and I.]

*_Excester_ is a fayre & large cittie, well walled & well traded, standing on the est syde of the river Ex, wherof it taketh name, which river springeth in Somersetshire, in Exmore, and kepeth his course southest to Exford, Winsford, & Exton, where it runneth towards the south, taking in certayne waters on both sydes, entreth into Devonshire at Exbridge from thence receiving waters on both sydes, it cometh to Teverton, where it receveth in the ryver of Loman, & so passeth to Bickley, Thewerton Nether Ex, & Stoke, where it receveth in the river of Columb, that cometh from Columbton & 2 myles lower another called Credy, that cometh from Crediton, and so arryeth at Excester, & from thence to

Exmister 3 myles of, a myle beneath which place it taketh in a river from the est, named Clist, and (begining to be somewhat broad) 2 myles lower, at Powderham Castle, taketh in another on the west syde, named Ken, & 2 myles from thence falleth into the sea at Exmouth

Chegford is 12 myles westward of Excester, on the est syde of Dartmore, & vppon the head of the river of Ting, which falleth into the sea at Tingmouth, 5 myles from Exmouth

Morton is 3 myles southest from Chegford

Chidley standeth vppon the said river of Ting, 7 myles southest from Morton, & as much southwest from Excester

Newton Bushell is 4 myles beneath Chidley, & 5 from Tingmouth

Ashburton is 5 myles west from Newton Bushell, vppon a small brooke, which a myle thence falleth into the Dart

Totnes standeth vppon the river of Dart (which springeth & ronneth through Dartmore), 5 myles south from Ashburton, & as farr west from Torrbay, and is one of the greatest townes in Deuonshire

Dartmouth standeth vppon the said river of Dart, 7 myles southest from Totnes & within 2 myles of the sea

Kingsbridge is 8 myles directly west from Dartmouth, vppon the head of *[leaf 14] a creek, which 4 myles thence falleth into the sea, & is called Saltcomb Hauen

Modbery is 5 myles northwest from Kingsbridge

Brent is 4 myles northest from Modbery, & 3 directly west from Totnes

Plimton standeth 9 myles directly west from Brent, & 3 est from Plimmouth, vppon a creek, which falleth into the hauen at Plimmouth

Plimmouth standeth on a pininsula within the hauen of Plimmouth, at the very furthest corner of Deuonshire, next to Cornwall. The cheiffest river that falleth into Plimmouth Hauen is the Tamer, which parteth Deuonshire & Cornwall a sunder, all his course, which from the head vntill it ffall into the sea is about 35 myles

Tauestoke is 10 myles north from Plimmouth & within 3 myles of Cornwall, vppon a small river named Tau, which falleth into the Tamer

Liston is 8 myles north from Tauestoke, on the west syde of Deuonshire, within 4 myles of Launston, in Cornwall

Okehampton standeth est from Liston 12 myles, vppon the head of a river named Oke, which springeth in Dartmore, & ronneth to Torrington & Bidiford, and lastly falleth into the Taw

Crediton (comonly called *Kirton*) is 12 myles est from Okehampton, & about 8 from Excester, vppon a small river named Credy, which ronneth into the Ex

Bow standeth in the very middest of Deuonshire, 5 myles from Crediton, & 7 from Okehampton, vppon the head of a small brook which ronneth into the Taw

Chimligh standeth 7 or 8 myles north from Bow, vppon a small brooke, *[leaf 44] which not farr from thence falleth into the Taw

Hatherley is 8 myles southwest from Chimligh, & as much northwest from Bow, 5 myles north from Okehampton

Houlsworthy standeth on the west syde of Deuonshire, within 3 myles of Cornwall, 10 myles from Hatherley, & 9 north from Liston

Harton standeth on the very northwest corner of Deuonshire, within two myles of the Severne Sea, & lyke distance from Cornwall

Torrington standeth on the est syde of the river of Oke, 8 myles north from Hatherley, & 4 from Bidiford

Bidiford standeth on the west side of the said river, 4 myles north from Torrington, & within 2 myles of the sea

Barstable standeth on the est side of the river Taw, 6 myles est from Bidiford, and was in tymes past a brave towne, with 4 gates, but now the suburbes are bigger then the towne

Ilfarcomb standeth on the Severne Sea syde, 7 myles north from Barstable

Combmerton standeth also on the Seaverne Sea syde, 4 myles estwards from Ilfarcomb

Moulton is 7 myles southest from Barstable, & vppon a small brook called Moule which springeth in Exmore, and falleth into the Taw

Baunton lyeth on the est syde of Deuonshire within two myles of Somersetshire, about 12 myles est from Moulton, & vppon a litle brooke, which not farr of, falleth into the Ex

Tiverton standeth vppon the river of Ex, 5 myles southward from Baunton, & 12 north from Excester

Columbton standeth vppon the river of Columb, 5 myles southest from Tiverton

Bradninch standeth also vppon the said Columb, 2 myles beneath Columbton

Autre standeth vppon a small river named Autre 8 myles est from Excester, & 4 from Honiton

Honiton standeth vppon the said river of Autre, 4 myles northest from Autre towne & 5 northwest from Culliton

Sidmouth standeth on the sea syde, on the mouth of a small creeke called Sid, distant from Autre southwards 4 or 5 myles

Culliton is 6 myles northest from Sidmouth & 7 est from Autre, and standeth vppon a small brook called Cully, which two myles thence falleth into the sea at Axmouth

Axminster standeth vppon the said river of Ax, on the very east corner of Deuonshire with[in] a myle of Dorcetshire, 4 myles northest from Culliton

About 3 myles est from Axminster, lyeth a round peece of Deuonshire, 3 myles long & 2 myles brode, which is compassed round about with Dorcetshire, saving on the north syde it hath Somersetshire, from the which it is seperated by the said river of Ax

[leaf 46 contains Coats of Arms, see Plate VII Nos 1 to 8]

CORNWALL

Cornwall is the vttermost part westward of all England, and lyeth lyke a promontory, or rather isthumus, for it hath the sea on ech syde & round about it, saving on the est end where it is seperated from Deuonshire by the river of Tamer, as before hath byn declared. It is full 60 myles long, but what it hath in length, it wanteth in breadth, yet at the est end where it ioyneth vppon Deuonshire, it is 40 myles brode, or 38 at the least, but the more westward it goeth the narrower yt is, so that about the middest it is not above 20 myles brode and last of all, not passing 5 myles. Although this countrey be but sandy & barren in comparison of other shyres, yet in some respects it passeth any of them as plentiousnes of tinne, flish and commodious havens for shipps. In the same I flynd to be 21 market townes the which I will name in order as they lye beginning at the est, & so passing along the south coast to the west end, and then on the north syde back agayne to the est and it hath about 266 parish churches.

Launston is of some accompted for the cheiffest towne in Cornwall because the Sessions and law matters are kept there. It is a prety walled towne, standing on the est end of the countrey within litle more then a myle of Deuonshire, and vppon a small river named Kensy, which 2 myles from thence falleth into the Tamer

Saltash standeth vppon the said river of Tamer, 15 myles directly south from Launston & 3 west from Plimmouth

Liskard standeth vpp into the meane land, 10 myles northwest from Saltash, & 6 from the sea syde

Low (which to be written trewly as it is pronounced) ought to be written *Lu*, standeth vppon the mouth of the river Low, 6 myles south from Liskerd

Foy is a brave towne, standing on the mouth of the river of Foy, within a myle of the sea, which is there called Foy Hauen, & is distant from Low directly west 6 myles Of the gallants of Foy, & of the'xploites which they did on the sea, especially with them of Rye & Winchilsey, I could say somwhat, if I meant not to be breeff

Lestethiell standeth vppon the said river of Foy, 5 myles north from Foy towne, & 3 south from Bodman

Bodman is accompted the greatest towne in Cornwall, and standeth in the *[leaf 47b] middest of the countrey, ffor it hath the sea on ech syde within 10 myles, and is 3 myles south from Lestethiell, & 7 northwest from Liskerd

Grampound standeth vppon the river of Fale, which falleth into Falmouth Hauen (the greatest hauen in Cornwall), distant westward from Foy 10 myles, & from Lestethiell vj

Tregny standeth in Roseland, and vppon the said river of Fale, 2 myles southwest & beneath Grampound

Truro is accompted the cheiffest Towne in all Cornwall for traffik of marchandize, and standeth on a peninsula, at the head of one of the armes of Falmouth Hauen, from Tregny & Grampound lyke distance of 6 myles

Tregunian standeth at the confluence of the 2 great waters, that which cometh from Truro, and the Fale, which cometh from Tregny, 4 myles from the one & as many from the other

Perin standeth on the west syde, and vppon a branch of Falmouth Hauen, distant ffrom Tregunian, directly west, 4 myles

*Helston is one of the greatest townes in Cornwall, and the place cheiffly *[leaf 48] for coynage of all Cornish tinne (although they coyne both at Truro & Lestethiell), and standeth in the countrey called Menege (which is a peninsula 10 myles long & 7 brode), and vppon a river named Loo, which some call Loo poole, because it is broder within then it is at the very mouth, but from the head vntill it come to Helston, it is called Cohor This towne is 6 myles directly west from Perin, and 3 from the meane sea

Pensanc standeth on the west syde of Mounts Bay, ten myles northwest from Helston, 2 from St Michaells Mount, and 4 on this syde St Buriens, which St Burien is iiij myles from the Landes End

St Tees lyeth on the north syde of Cornwall on the sea syde, and at the entring of a bay called St Tee's bay, 12 myles from the Lands end, & 5 northest from Pensance

St Columb (called great St Columb, for differrence of litle St Columb not farr of) is 24 myles directly est from St Tees, 8 from Bodman, and vppon a small brook, which falleth into the sea

Padstow standeth on the west syde of a great river, which some call Helan, others Dunmere, but comonly Padstow Water, & is 6 myles northest from St Columb, & 2 from the sea Foure myles from Padstow is a bridge over the said river, called Wadbridge, which is the greatest bridge in Cornwall

*Camelford standeth vppon the head of the said river of Helan, 9 myles directly *[leaf 48b] est from Padstow, & 10 from Launston

Treuenna standeth on the sea syde, 4 myles from Camelford, & 6 est of Padstow Hauen A litle myle from Treuenna is Tintagell, which hath a castell standing in the sea, very strongly on a rock, called Tintagell Castell

Boscastle is 3 myles est from Treuenna, vppon the mouth of a small creek, not farr from the sea

Stratton standeth on the northest corner of Cornwall, 10 myles from Boscastle, vj from Launston, within 2 myles of Deuonshire, & as much from the sea It is compassed on ech syde with two small brookes which meet there, and geveth name to all the Hundred where it standeth, called Stratton Hundred

Now I have gone as farr westward as I can on the south syde of the river of Thamise. It cometh best to purpose to begynn agayne at the est, and on the north syde of the same river with the countrey of Essex.

[leaf 49v contains Coats of Arms of the Earls of Essex: see Plate X.]

*ESSEX

Essex taketh name of the Est Saxons, which was in tymes past a kingdome, contayning, not only Essex, but also Midlesex, and part of Hartfordshire. On the est it hath the sea, on the south it is parted from Kent by the river of Thamise, on the west yt hath Midlesex and Hartfordshire, on the northwest corner it toucheth on Cambridgeshire & hath Suffolk on the north. The length therof is, est and west, 40 myles, the breadth 35, and the compass round about is about 120 myles. In which countrey (besydes the cittie of Colchester) there is 19 market townes (or 18 as some reakon, which leave out Harwich), and it hath 415 parish churches, besydes villages, gentlemens howses & castells.

[The ten under of this page is occupied with a View of Colchester: see Plate XX.]

Colchester is a most ancient cittie, standing on the northest corner of Essex, vppon a river named Colney, which springeth in the south syde of Essex, about 16 myles northwest from Colchester, and falleth into the sea 3 myles beneath Brikelsey. It is called in Brittish, Caercoill, and was founded by Coill, King of Brittains. It hath within the walles, a marvelous old castell, standing on a hill, & 15 churches, most part with broade or square steples. There can no shipps come to the towne, but to Brikelsey, which is 4 myles from thence.

Hamington standeth on the south syde of the river of Clare (or Stoure as some call it) which parteth Suffolk from Essex, 6 myles from Colchester, & as farr from Harwich.

Harwich standeth at the mouth of the sud river, where the river of Orwell (which cometh from Ipswich) falleth into the sea & is there called Orwell Hauen. It is a prety litle towne, walled on the north syde, and although it be no market towne, yet it may passe amongst them.

Maldon standeth on the south syde of the river that cometh from Chelmsford (which some call Chelmer), distant 9 myles est from Chelmsford, & 10 south from Colchester.

Chelmsford is of some accompted the shyre towne of Essex, because the Sessions and law matters are kept there, and standeth almost in the very middest of the countrey. Three myles beyond Chelmsford is Newhall, a manor place of the kings, which now belongeth to the Erle of Sussex.

Brentwood is 15 myles from London & in the way from Colchester.

Rumford standeth in Hauering Liberty, in the way betwene Brentwood & London. Hauering is the kings howse, which is 2 myles north from Rumford. Hauering Libertie is 4 myles ech way.

Horndon on the Hill standeth within 2 myles of the Thamise.

Beherrair is 4 myles north from Horndon.

Ralegh standeth in Rochford Hundred, 3 myles from Ligh, & as many from Rochford.

Barking standeth within a myle of the Thamise, and about 6 myles est from London.

Waltham Cross (which some call Waltham Abbay) is 12 myles north from London, and standeth on the est syde of the river of Lea, which parteth Essex from Midlesex.

Hatfield Brodok standeth on the west end of Essex, 10 myles northest from Waltham, and 5 from Dunmow.

Halden (comonly called *Saffon Halden*, because of the great abundance of

* "Is is" in the MS.

safron *which* groweth thereabout) is 10 myles north from Hatfeild, and standeth on *the* northwest corner of Essex, *within* 4 myles of Cambridgeshire

Thaxted standeth on *the* head of *the* river Chelmer, 5 myles southest from Safron Walden

Dunmow standeth vppon *the* said river of Chelmer, 5 myles from Thaxted, & 10 northwest from Chelmsford. He that is maried, & doth not repent hym therof within the first yeare & day, may come to Dunmow & fetch a flitch of bacon

Braintree is 6 myles est from Dunmow, & as many west from Coxhall, halfe way betwene both

Halsted standeth vppon *the* river of Colney, 8 myles west from Colchester, & 5 northest from Braintree

*_Coggeshall_ (comonly called *Coxhall*) is 5 myles southest from Halsted, and halff *[leaf 51*b*]* way betwene Braintre & Colchester, to say 6 myles from ech. It standeth on a river named Blackwater, *which* falleth into *the* Chelmer not farr fro*m* Maldon

Witham is xj myles from Colchester, & 7 ffrom Chelmesford, in the way to London

Forrests in Essex

Waltham Forrest, by Waltham

Hatfeild Forrest, by Hatfeild Brodeoke, ys palled about, & is but two myles longe & one myle brode

*MIDDLESEX *[leaf 52]*

Middlesex taketh name of *the* Midlesaxons, & is *the* least shyre in England except Rutland. It hath on *the* est Essex (from *the which* it is seperated by *the* river of Lea), on *the* south it is devyded from Surrey by the river of Thamise, on *the* west from Buckinghamshire by *the* river of Coll, and hath Hartfordshyre on *the* north. The length therof is, from *the* est to *the* west, 18 myles, the breadth at both ends is 12 myles, but in *the* middest it is not passing 8 myles brode. In which countrey (besydes the roiall cittie of London) there is 3 market townes & 73 parish churches

[The Coat of Arms of the City of London occupies the rest of the page. see Plate I.]

*London (the cheiff & principall cittie in all England), although it be scituated in *[leaf 52*b*]* *the* province of Middlesex, yet it is a countie of it selff. This roiall & famous citty standeth on *the* north syde of the river of Thamise, which river is there a thousand foote brode, over which there is a goodly bridge of stone, which hath 20 arches, *that* are 60 foote in height, 30 in thicknes, & distant one from another 20 foote. On both sydes of the bridge are howses builded, in such sort that it seemeth rather a continuall street then a bridge. London is 3 myles long (accompting Westminster withall), and is two myles brode, reakoning Southwark & *the* bridge. It is devyded into 26 wardes, and hath 108 parish churches within the walles, and xj without *the* walles, but yet within the Liberties, which is in all 119

Westminster lyeth at *the* west end of London, lyke the suburbes, and was of late, by Quene Elizabeth, made a cittie. In the great church of St. Peter are the sepultures of dyvers kings & noblemen, and hard by is Westminster Hall

[A View of London is here inserted, but the folio is not counted. see Plate XXVIII.]

*Brainford is 8 myles west from London, and standeth vppon a small river *[leaf 53]* (which some call Brain) that there falleth into *the* Thamise

Stains standeth vppon the Thamise, 7 myles from Brainford, & 15 from London, & 3 myles from Colbrok in Buckinghamshire

Vxbridge standeth on *the* west end of Middlesex, and vppon the river of Coll, 6 myles north from Stanes, 3 from Colbroke, & 16 from London

In Middlesex standeth also Hampton Court vppon the Thamise, xj myles from London, & a myle from Kingston, which (as some say) is *the* fayrest howse that the

4

king hath. And in the northest corner of the countrey, hard by Waltham, is Enfeld Chase, where there is also a howse called Enfeld Howse.

*HARTFORDSHYRE

[A Coat of Arms is at the top—see Plate XIV., No. 1.]

Hartfordshire taketh name of the towne of Hartford, and hath on the est Essex, on the south Middlesex, on the west Buckinghamshire & Bedfordshire, and hath Cambridgshire on the north. It contayneth in length from the north to the south, 25 myles, and the breadth is 20 myles, in some places more, & in some lesse. In which countrey there is 17 market townes, & about 130 parish churches.

[leaf 54 has the number omitted, so 53, 54, 55.]

Hartford is an ancient towne & castell standing on ech syde of the river of Lea, distant 2 myles westward from Ware.

Ware standeth on the north syde of the said river, 20 myles north from London, and in the hygh way to London from the north countrey.

Hoddesdon is 3 myles from Ware, & 5 from Waltham, in London way also.

Bishoppshatfield is 5 myles southwest from Hartford, and as many est from St Albones. At this towne is a goodly howse of brick belonging to the king.

St. Albones is the fayrest & greatest towne in all the shyre, and standeth on a hill just 20 myles northwest from London, vppon the banck of a small river named Coll, which runneth to Colbrok. Not farr from St Albones stood the famous cittie of Verolanum[1] Verlancester, as yet is easely to be seene, which as some wryte was in the tyme of the Romains esteemed above London.

Barnet (otherwise called High Barnet, ffor differece of Est Barnet in Middlesex) standeth hard vppon Middlesex, halff way betwene St Albones & London, 10 myles from ech.

Watford standeth vppon the river of Coll 8 myles west from Barnet, & 6 south from St Albones.

Hemsted is 5 myles west from St Albones. Betwene Hemsted & Watford lyeth Kings-Langley, and not farr from thence Abbotts Langley.

Barkamsted (comonly called Great Barkamsted, ffor differece of Litle Barkamsted, not farr from Hartford) is 3 myles west from Hemsted.

Tring is 3 myles west of Barkamsted, and toucheth vppon Buckinghamshire.

Hitchin is xi myles north from St Albones, on the west syde of the shyre, within two myles of Bedfordshyre.

Baldock is 5 myles northest from Hitchin, and within two myles also of Bedfordshyre.

Roiston standeth on the very northend of the countrey, so that it toucheth vppon Cambridgeshire, and is 7 myles northest ffrom Baldock, & in London way from the north countrey.

Barkway is 3 myles southest from Roiston, & within two myles of Essex, in London way from Walsingham in Norfolk.

Buntingford is 6 myles from Roiston, & 7 ffrom Ware, in the way betwene them.

Puckrich (which some say was anciently called Pulcherchurch) is 3 myles from Buntingford, & 7 directly south from Barkway, 5 from Ware, and in the way betwene Barkway & Ware.

Bishopps-Startford standeth on the est syde of the countrey, within a myle of Essex, & vppon a river named Stoure, which a myle beneath this towne parteth Hartfordshire from Essex vntill it fall into the Lea & then it geveth over both name & office. This towne is 7 myles directly est from Puckrich.

[Leaf 56 contains Coats of Arms of the Earls and Dukes of Suffolk—see Plate XV., Nos. 12 to 15.]

[1] A word, probably *or*, seems to have been accidentally rubbed away.

*SUFFOLK

*[leaf 57]

Suffolk lyeth on *the* south part of that countrey which in tymes past was called the kingdome of Est England, and therof taketh name, ffor Suffolk or Southfolk is all one. This countrey of Suffolk hath on *the* est end the Germaine Occeane, on *the* south syde Essex, ffrom *the* which yt ys devyded by the river of Clare, which some call Stoure, on the west it hath Cambridgeshire, & Norfolk on *the* north. It contayneth in length, from Eston (which is the most estwards part of all England) to Newmarket in *the* west, 44 myles, and the breadth is 20 myles; but at *the* est end yt is 30 myles brode, and the compasse therof round about is 120 myles. In which countrey there is 25 market townes and 575 parish churches, besydes villages, gentlemens howses, & castells

*[Coat of Arms of the town of Ipswich at the top: see Plate I.]   *[leaf 57b]

Ipswich is *the* greatest towne in Suffolk, and one of the most famous townes in England at this present for trafike and other respects, and standeth in the southest corner of the countrey, vppon the river of Orwell, 7 myles from *the* sea. It hath xj churches in it

Nedham standeth vppon *the* said river of Orwell, 6 myles northwest from Ipswich

Stow standeth vppon *the* head of *the* said river of Orwell, 3 litle myles northwest from Needham, & in *the* very middest of Suffolk

Hadly is 7 myles directly south from Stow, vppon a small river, which 4 myles thence falleth into *the* Clare

Lancham standeth on *the* head of the same river, 6 myles northwest from Hadley

* *Sudbury* standeth vppon *the* river of Clare (that parteth Suffolk from Essex), 5 *[leaf 58] myles directly south from Lancham, & 6 southest from Clare

Clare is a towne & castell, standing vppon *the* fornamed river of Clare (which some call Stoure), 6 myles northwest from Sudbury. Of this towne did the Clares take name that were Erles of Glocester, whose issew in tyme ended in 3 doughters, whereof one was maried to John Burg, Erle of Vlster, in Ireland, and his issew also ended in a doughter named Elizabeth maried to Leonell, second sonne to K Edward 3, who by her was Erle of Vlster, & was after created Duke of Clarence. And this was *the* first originall or begining of *the* said Dukedome

Haverill standeth on *the* head of *the* said river of Clare, & on the very southwest corner of Suffolk, 4 myles directly west from Clare. It toucheth on Essex, & is within a myle of Cambridgeshyre

Newmarket standeth on *the* very west end of *the* countrey, and so nigh to Cambridgeshyre that (as I judge) some part of the towne standeth in the said shyre. It is 9 myles from Haverill, and 7 southest from Ely

Mildnall is 6 myles north of Newmarket, and two myles from Cambridgeshyre

**Brandon* (which some call Brandon Ferry) standeth vppon the river of Litle *[leaf 58b] Ouse, which parteth Norfolk from Suffolk, 6 myles northest from Mildnall, & 5 west from Thetford in Norfolk

Bury (which is also called St Edmunds Bury) is accompted the shyre towne of Suffolk, because the Sessions & Assyses are kept there, and is a proper towne, standing on the head of a small river or brooke, which ronneth from thence to Mildnall, & so falleth into *the* Great Ouse 2 myles beneath Ely. This towne is 9 myles north from Clare, 10 est from Newmarket, & as many west from Stow

Wulpet is 6 myles est from Bury, & 4 from Stow

Buddesdale is 7 myles north from Stow, and within 2 myles of Lopham Ford, where Norfolk parteth from Suffolk

Aye is 5 myles est from Buddesdale

Debenham is 4 myles directly south from Aye, and standeth on *the* head of a small river, which falleth into *the* sea at Baudsey. Fyve myles northest from this towne is Framlingham Castell, standing vppon the head of Orford River

Bungay standeth vppon the river of Waueney, which parteth Norfolk from Suffolk, 9 myles north from Framingham Castell, & as many northest from Aye

Beckles standeth vppon the same river, 4 myles estward from Bungay

Lestoft standeth on the sea syde, in a peninsula (named Louingland, or Low England as some terme it), 6 myles south from Yermouth, & 7 est from Beckles

Sowould (comonly called Sowl) standeth also vppon the sea syde 8 myles south from Lestoft, on the mouth of a small river, which there maketh a prety hauen

Halesworth is 6 miles directly west from Sowould, vppon the head of the said river which ronneth to Sowld

Dunwich standeth on the sea syde, two myles south from Sowould, and was in tymes past a famous cittie and Bishoppuck (which Bishoppuck was after translated to Elmeham, from thence to Thetford, and lastly to Norwich) But now the sea hath eaten most part of the towne away, so that there remayneth but 3 churches therein, where once were 12

Saxmundham is 6 myles southwest from Dunwich, 4 from the sea, & 5 est from Framingham

Aldeborough standeth on the sea syde, 7 myles south from Dunwich

Orford towne & castell do stand at the point of the land called Orfordness, two myles from Aldeborough, & 10 or 12 myles from Harwich

Woodbridge is 5 myles northest from Ipswich, and standeth within a myle of a small river (which some call Deue) that cometh from Debenham, & falleth into the sea at Baudsey, making there a prety hauen, called Baudsey Hauen

[leaf 60 contains Coats of Arms of the Dukes of Norfolk see Plate XII, Nos 10 to 13]

NORFOLK

Norfolk lyeth on the north part of that countrey which in old tyme was called Est England, and hath the sea almost round about it, saving on the south it hath Suffolk, on the west Cambridgeshire & a peece of Lincolneshire The length therof is, from Yermouth in the est to Walpoole in Marshland in the west 50 myles, the breadth 30, and the compass round about is about 130 myles In which countrey (besydes the cittie of Norwich) there is 26 market townes, and hath to the nomber of 625 parish churches, besydes villages which have no churches, townshipps, gentlemens howses, and castells

[The remainder of this page is occupied with 2 Coats of Arms see Plate XIII, Nos 15 and 16]

[leaf 61b contains a View of Norwich see Plate XXIII]

Norwich ys the cheiffe cittie in Norfolk, and the third cittie in England, to say, the greatest saving London & York It hath 25 parish churches, & all within the walles, also an ancient castell standing on a hill, almost in the very middest of the cittie Through the citty passeth a brave river, named Yei, which about 13 myles thence falleth into the sea at Yermouth

Windondham (comonly called Windham) is an ancient & great towne, standing 6 myles southwest from Norwich

Hingham is 4 myles westward from Windham

Buckenham (comonly called New Buckenham, ffor diffience of Old Buckenham hard by it) is 5 myles directly south from Hingham

Herling (comonly called Est Herling, for diffience of West Herling hard by) is 3 myles southwest from Buckenham

Thetford is [an] ancient towne, having yet a maior and was in tymes past a bishoppuck, ffrom whence it was translated to Norwich and standeth vppon the river of Litle Ouse, which parteth Norfolk from Suffolk, 6 myles southwest from Est Herling

Watton is 9 myles directly north from Thetford

Dereham (comonly called Est Dereham, for diffience of West Dereham not farr from Downeham) is 5 myles north from Watton, & 10 west from Norwich

Swafham is 7 myles westwards from Est Dereham

Downham standeth on the est syde of the river of Great Ouse, 9 myles west southwest from Swafham

Lynn is the bravest towne in Norfolk next Norwich, and standeth on the est syde of the said river of Great Ouse, 8 myles north from Downcham, & within 3 myles of the Washes, which are betwene Lincolnshire & Norfolk. Old Lynn standeth on the other syde of the river, in Marshland

Snetsham is 8 myles north from Lynn, and within 2 myles of the Washes, in the northwest corner of Norfolk *[leaf 63]

Burnham is 7 myles northest from Snetsham, & 2 myles from the sea. It is comonly called Burnham Market, because of dyvers other townes therabouttes lying together, as Burnham Debdale, Burnham Over, Burnham Norton, Burnham Sutton, & Burnham Thorp

Walsingham is one of the greatest townes in Norfolk, and standeth 6 myles southest from Burnham Market, & 4 myles ffrom the sea

Fakenham is 3 myles directly south from Walsingham

Clay standeth on the north syde of Norfolk, on the mouth of a small river within a myle of the sea, & 5 myles northest from Walsingham

Holt is two myles south from Clay

Cromer standeth on the sea syde, 6 myles est from Clay

Repeham standeth into the land, 10 myles south from Cromer, & 8 northwest from Norwich

Caston is two myles northest from Repeham

Alesham is 2 myles northest from Caston, vppon a small river which falleth into the Yer, hard by Yermouth

Walsham (comonly called North Walsham, for diffrence of South Walsham, 8 *[leaf 63b] myles southest from thence) standeth 4 myles northest from Alesham, & 3 from the sea

Wursted is 2 myles south southest from North Walsham

Hickling is 4 myles est from Wursted, & 2 myles from the sea

Yermouth is a proper walled towne, standing 9 myles southest from Hickling, vppon the mouth of the river Yer, which a little mile southest from thence falleth into the sea, and yet on the est syde of the towne a man may almost throw a stone into the sea

Harleston standeth on the river of Waueney, which parteth Norfolk from Suffolk, 16 myles southwest from Yermouth, & 4 from Bungay in Suffolk

Dis standeth vppon the said river of Waueney, 6 myles southwest from Harleston, & 4 myles from Loppamford. Three myles from Dis, & as many from Buckenham, & lyke distance from Herling, standeth Kenningale Castell

*CAMBRIDGESHIRE *[leaf 64]

[Two Coats of Arms at top see Plate XIII, Nos 1 and 2]

Cambridgeshire is cut in two by the river of Ouse, & as it were into two countreis The north part wherof is called the Isle of Ely, which is as bigg, or rather bigger, then that part of Cambridgeshire. But in nomber of townes & villages Cambridgeshire passeth the Ile of Ely 3 tymes. This shyre (accompting the Ile of Ely therwith, for it is all in Cambridgeshyre) is in length, north & south, about 38 myles, in breadth, 10, 15, & in some places, 20 myles. It hath on the est Norfolk & Suffolk, on the southest Essex, on the south Hartfordshire, on the southwest Bedfordshire, on the west Huntingtonshyre, on the northwest a peece of Northamptonshire, and on the north Lincolnshire. In which countrey (besydes Cambridge & Ely) there is 4 other market townes, and 163 parish churches, or thereaboutts

[leaf 64b contains a View of Cambridge see Plate XXIII]

Cambrige (called in Brittish, Caergrant, & by the Saxons, Grantbridge) is a *[leaf 65] famous towne & florishing Vniversyte, standing vppon the river Granta, which ronneth through the middest of the same shyre, and falleth into the Ouse 3 myles south of Ely. It is 10 myles southeast from Huntington, & as many south from Ely.

Linton (or *Lenton* as some call it) toucheth vppon Essex, & is 7 myles southeast from Cambridge.

Reche is 7 myles northest from Cambridge, and within 3 myles of Suffolk, vppon a creeke which is diggedd from the Ouse to the towne, almost 2 myles long, & is 5 myles from Ely. Betwene this towne & Ely are two meares. Stretham Mere on the left hand, which is a myle long & halffe a myle brode, taking name of Stretcham hard by, and Seham Mere on the right hand, which is somewhat bigger, and taketh name of Seham therby.

[leaf 65]

Ely ys a bishopps seat, standing on the west syde of the river of Great Ouse aforsaid, & in the Ile of Ely, which Isle of Ely is not one only Isle but consisteth of many Ilandes, 15 in nomber at the least, seperated one from another by rivers, waters, or dyches, and all called the Isle of Ely.

Litleport standeth in the said Ile of Ely, 4 myles directly north from Ely, & within a myle of the northwest corner of Suffolk.

Wisbich standeth also in the said Ile 10 myles north from Litleport, & hard vppon Norfolk.

[leaf 66r contains Coats of Arms of Earls of Huntington - see Plate XII, Nos 5 to 9.]

[leaf 66v]

HUNTINGTONSHYRE

Huntingtonshire[1] ys one of the least shyres in England. It is in proportion 4 square, or rather 4 cornered, lyke a diamond vppon a payre of cardes, being not above 12 myles from the one syde to the other. But the longest way is from the north corner to the south, which is 20 myles, and from the est corner to the west is about 16 myles, so that it is about halff so bigg as Cambridgshire or Northamptonshire, and is environed round about with the said 2 shyres, saving on the southwest it toucheth on Bedfordshyre. In which countrey there is 5 market townes & 78 parish churches.

[l of 67]

Huntington ys the towne which geveth name to all the whole countrey, and standeth on the north bank of the river of Ouse, 10 myles northwest from Cambridge, 12 northest from Bedford, and within 3 myles of Cambrigeshyre.

Saint Ives (which to be written as it is spoken, ought rather to be written *St Tyues*) standeth vppon the sayd river of Ouse, 3 myles beneath, & directly est from Huntington.

Saint Neot, or *St Edes* (comonly called *St Needs*) standeth also vppon the said river of Ouse 6 myles above, & almost south from Huntington, & hard by Bedfordshire.

Kimbalton is 7 myles west from Huntington, and within a myle of Bedfordshire.

Yaxley standeth in the north corner of the shyre 10 myles north from Huntington, a myle from Stilton, within two myles of Northamptonshire, & within 3 of Cambridgshire.

[leaf 67v contains 5 Cts of Arms - see Plate VII, Nos 13 to 17.]

[leaf 68]

BEDFORDSHIRE

Bedfordshire is not much bigger then Huntingtonshire, but it is more inhabited, & better replenished with townes. It hath Huntingtonshire on the northest, Cambridgeshire on the est, Hartfordshire on the southest, Buckinghamshire on the west, & on the northwest it toucheth on Northamptonshire. The length therof is from the north to the south 24 myles, and the breadth in the middest (which is the brodest place) is 14 myles. In which countrey (besides Bedford) there are 9 market townes, & 113 parish churches.

[The lower part of the page contains the Coat of Arms of the town of Bedford - See Plate I.]

[1] *added* in the MS

*Bedford is a proper towne, walled about, with iij churches therein, and standeth *[leaf 68]
on the north syde of the river of Ouse, about 12 myles southwest ffrom Huntington

Potton is 7 myles est from Bedford, & within a myle of Cambridgeshyre

Bigleswade is 2 myles south from Potton

Shefford is 3 myles south southwest from Bigleswade, and standeth betwene 2
rivers, which meet there, & so do ronne from thence in one chanell to Bigleswade,
& 4 myles beneath Bedford do fall into the Ouse

Anthill is 4 myles west from Shefford, & 5 directly south from Bedford

*Woburn is 4 myles southwest from Anthill, and within 2 myles of Buck- *[leaf 69]
inghamshire

Tuddington is 3 myles southest from Woburn, & 4 directly south from Anthill

Leghton standeth on a small river, which there parteth Bedfordshire from Buckinghamshire, iiij myles southwest from Tuddington, which river ronneth from thence
to Fenny Stratford, & falleth into the Ouse at Newport Panell

Dunstable standeth in London way from Coventry, 5 myles southest from
Leghton, & 30 from London

Luton is 3 myles estwards from Dunstable, & within a myle of Hartfordshyre

[leaf 69b contains Coats of Arms of Earls of Northampton see Plate X]

*NORTHAMPTONSHIRE *[leaf 70]

Northamptonshire is as bigg as both Bedfordshire & Huntingtonshire, and
stretcheth in length from the southwest to the northest, hauing on the southest
syde Cambridgeshire, Huntingtonshire, Bedfordshire, & Buckinghamshire, on the
northwest it hath Lincolnshire, Rutland, Leicestershire, & Warwikshire, and on the
southwest corner it toucheth on Oxfordshyre. The length from the southwest to
the northest (to say) from Banbury, in Oxfordshire, to Crowland, in Lincolnshire,
is 42 myles, and the breadth in the middest is 18 myles. But the more northward
it goeth the narrower it is, so that in some places it is not passing 4 myles brode
In which countrey is 10 market townes & 326 parish churches

[The lower part of the page contains the Coat of Arms of the town of Northampton see Plate I]

*Northampton is a brave towne, walled about, with 5 churches therein, and *[leaf 70b]
standeth vppon the river of Nine, distant 12 myles directly north from Buckingham,
& as many south from Herborow, in Leicestershire

Dauentree is 8 myles west from Northampton, & within 2 myles of Warwickshire, in London way from Coventree

Brakley standeth on the south end of the shyre, hard vppon Buckinghamshire,
vppon the head of the river Ouse, 4 myles west from Buckingham, & 6 south from
Towcester

Towcester standeth in London way, 10 myles southest from Dauentrie, and 6
south from Northampton

Wellingborow standeth vppon the river of Nine, 7 myles northest from
Northampton

Higham Ferries standeth on the est syde of the said river of[1] Nine, 3 myles
northest from Wellingborow

Thrapston standeth also on the est syde of the said river, 4 myles north from
Higham Ferries

Kettering standeth in the middest of the shyre, 10 myles north from Northampton, & 5 west from Thrapston

*Oundley is compassed almost round about with the said river of Nine, & is 5 *[leaf 71]
myles north northwest from Thrapston, & 3 south from Fodringhay Castell. At
the College of Fodringhay are dyvers noblemen buried, as, namely, Edmund of
Langley, Duke of York, Edward, Duke of York, his sonne, who was slaine at the
battaill of Azincourt, Ric D of York, father to K E 4, and others

Peterborow standeth vppon the said river of Nine, in the northest corner of the

---

[1] The word of is repeated in the MS

shyre, & at *the* meeting of Cambridgeshire, Huntingtonshire, & Northamptonshire, *which* river there devydeth it selfe into sundry branches, compassing & going through the Ile of Ely, and is distant 9 myles northest from Oundley, 8 southest ffrom Stamford, in Lincolneshire, & 4 north from Yaxley, in Huntingtonshire. It was made a bishoppricke by K. H. 8.

Forrests in Northamptonshire

Whitlewood Forrest, hard by Towcester, wherein standeth the Kings manor place of Grafton.

Saucy Forrest, betwene Stonistretford & Northampton.

Rokingham Forrest, wherby standeth the Castell of Rokingham, hard by Rutland.

*BUCKINGHAMSHYRE

[Three Coats of Arms at top — see Plate XIII, Nos. 5 to 7.]

Buckinghamshire stretcheth from *the* Thamise till it come as farre as Northampton. It hath on *the* est syde Bedfordshire, Hartfordshire, & Middlesex, on *the* south end it is devyded from Surrey & Barkshyre by the river of Thamise, on *the* west syde it hath Oxfordshyre, & on *the* northwest end Northamptonshyre. The length is from the Thamise to *the* northend about 40 myles, the breadth 14, 12, & in some places but 8 myles. In which countrey there is xj market townes and 185 parish churches.

*[At the top of the page is the Coat of Arms of the town of Buckingham — see Plate I.]

Buckingham standeth in *the* northwest corner of *the* shyre, vppon the river of Ouse, within 2 myles of Oxfordshyre, & within 3 myles of Northamptonshire, which river of Ouse springeth not farr from Brackley, in Northamptonshire, and passeth through Buckinghamshire to Buckingham, Stonistretford, Newport Panell, & Oulney, through Bedfordshire to Bedford, through Huntingtonshire to St Needs, Huntington, & St Tyues, through Cambrigeshire to Ely, through Norfolk to Downeham & Linn, where not farr of it falleth into *the* Washes.

Stonistretford standeth on *the* est syde of *the* said river of Ouse (which there parteth Buckinghamshire from Northamptonshire), about 6 myles northest from Buckingham, & as many from Towcester, in London way from Couentrie.

Newport Paganell (comonly called *Newport Panell*) standeth vppon *the* said river, 4 myles from Stonistretford.

Oulney standeth also vppon *the* said river, in *the* furthermost corner of *the* shyre, 5 myles north from Newport Panell, & halff way betwene Northampton & Bedford, 7 myles from ech.

Winslow is 6 myles southest from Buckingham.

Iuingo standeth on *the* est syde of *the* shyre, within a myle of Hartfordshire, 4 myles southwest from Dunstable, in Bedfordshire, & 3 north from Tring, in Hartfordshire. Foure myles southest from Iuingo is *the* Kings howse called Ashridge, but (as I thinck) part of *the* towne standeth in Hartfordshire.

Ailsbury standeth in *the* middest of *the* shire, vppon *the* head of *the* river of Tame, 6 myles from the towne of Tame, & as many from Iuingo. Here *the* Sessions are comonly kept.

Agmundsham (comonly called *Amersham*) is 10 myles southest from Ailesbury.

Wickam (comonly called *High Wickam*, for difference of *West Wickam* not farr of) standeth vppon *the* head of a small brook, which falleth into *the* Thamise at Hedsor, and is 4 myles southwest from Amersham.

Beaconsfild is 4 myles southest from Wickam, & as many south from Amersham (ffor these 3 townes do stand in triangle, and betwene them is a village called Pen, hard by which lyeth a peece of Hartfordshire of 2 myles long, & one mile broad, & all enclosed within Buckinghamshire.

Colbroke standeth in *the* south corner of the shyre, vppon the river Coll, 3 myles from Windsor, 3 from Stanes, & 16 west from London.

DESCRIPTION OF ENGLAND

Forrests in Buckinghamshire

Bernwood Forrest, on *the* west syde   Whaddon Chase, by Fennystretford

*OXFORDSHIRE

[Two Coats of Arms at top—see Plate XI, Nos 13 and 14]

Next to Buckinghamshire on *the* west lyeth Oxfordshire, which is in proportion much lyke a shoulder of mutton, ffor it is 30 myles brode at *the* west end, and *the* further it goeth toward *the* southest the narrower it is, so *that* in some places it is but 10, 8, 6, or 4 myles brode, and *the* longest length is from *the* southest to the northwest, which is from the Thamise at Reding till it come 5 myles beyonde Banbury, which is about 40 myles, and hath Buckinghamshire on *the* est, Barkshire on *the* south (from *the* which it is seperated by *the* river of Thamise), on *the* west Glocestershire & Warwikshire, & hath Northamptonshyre on the northest corner In which countrey (besydes the cittie & Vniuersity of Oxford) there is 9 market townes, and 208 parish churches

*[View of Oxford at top—see Plate XXIV]

Oxford is a braue cittie, walled about rounde, much lyke vnto Canterbury, and a florishing Vniuersytie of all kind of learning, standing on *the* south syde of the shyre, where the river of Cherwell falleth into *the* Thamise

Whitney is 8 myles west from Oxford, and standeth vppon a small river named Windrush, which at Newbridge, 4 myles thence, falleth into *the* Thamise

Burford standeth vppon *the* same river, 5 myles west from Whitney, and within 2 myles of Glocestershire

Woodstock is 6 myles northwest from Oxford, where there is a roiall manor & park belonging to *the* King

Chipping-Norton is 7 myles northwest from Woodstock, & 5 est from Stow on *the* Would, which is in Glocestershire

Banbury is 12 myles north from Woodstock, and standeth on *the* north corner of Oxfordshyre, vppon the river of Cherwell, that there parteth it from Northamptonshire, which river ronneth through *the* middest of Oxfordshire, & falleth into *the* Thamise at Oxford   At this towne are excellent good cheeses made, but I did never see any thick ynowgh

Burcester (comonly called *Bicster*) standeth on *the* est syde of *the* countrey, 12 myles southest from Banbury, 6 southwest from Buckingham, and within 3 myles of Buckinghamshire

Tame toucheth on Buckinghamshire, & is 10 myles southest from Bicster, & as many est northest from Oxford, and standeth vppon *the* river of Tame, *that* falleth into *the* Ise at Dorchester, 7 myles beneath Oxford, and there causeth *the* name of Thamise   Which Dorchester was in tymes past a proper towne, & a Bishopprick, vntill it was translated from thence to Lincolne

Watlington is 6 myles south from Tame, and as many northest from Dorchester

Henley standeth vppon *the* Thamise, 7 myles southest from Watlington, & 5 north from Reding

Forrests

There is but one forrest in Oxfordshire, which is called Wichwood Forrest, lying betwene Woodstock & Burford

[leaf 75b contains Coats of Arms of Earls of Gloucester—see Plate XV]

*GLOCESTERSHYRE

Glocestershire taketh name of *the* cittie of Glocester, and contayneth in length, from Bristow in *the* south end till it come within a myle of Stretford vppon Avon, in Warwikshire, which is about 46 myles: and *the* breadth, from Lechlade in the est to Monmouth in Wales, is about 34 myles. It hath Warwikshire on *the* north end, Oxfordshyre & a litle peece of Barkshire on *the* est, Wiltshire on *the* southest, Monmouthshyre & Herefordshire on *the* west, & Worcestershire on the northwest. In which countrey, besydes the two citties of Bristow & Glocester, there is 21 market townes, & 314 parish churches: of which nomber 3 market townes & 48 parish churches do stand on *the* west syde of the river of Severn.

Glocester is a famous cittie standing vppon *the* said river of Severne, called in British Caerglow, and was founded by Claudius the Emprour, as some wryte, who named it Claudia Cestria.

[The lower part of the page contains a Coat of Arms—see Plate XIV, No. 2]

[leaf 77 contains a View of Bristol—see Plate XXV.]

Bristow is one of *the* greatest & famousest citties in England, and standeth vppon the river of Avon, which 4 myles thence falleth into *the* Severn, over which river there is a fayre bridge of stone, with houses on ech syde lyke London Bridge, & almost half so long: although it have but 4 arches, so that one quarter of the cittie standeth in Somersetshire; but the Bristollians will be a shyre of them selves, & not accompted in any other shyre. In the est end of *the* cittie is the castell, which they confess to stand in Glocestershyre. There is no dunghill in all *the* cittie, nor any sinck *that* cometh from any howse, but all convaid vnder *the* ground, neither vse they any cartes in their streetes, but all sleades. There is in *the* cittie 20 ffayre churches, whereof 18 are parish churches.

Cheltenham standeth by Glocester Marsh, 6 myles northest from Gloucester.

Tewksbury is a proper town, standing 7 myles north from Glocester, where the river of Avon (which cometh from Warwik) falleth into *the* Severn, hard vppon Worcestershyre, and was founded by Robert Fitzhamon, Erle of Glocester, who is there buried, & divers other noblemen & princes, as Henry, Duke of Warwik, an. 1446, Edward, Prince of Wales an. 1471, sonne to K. H. 6, George, Duke of Clarence, Edward, L. Spencer, John L. Wenlock, & others.

Winchcomb is 6 myles est from Tewksbury & 4 northest from Chiltenham, and a myle thence is a great park wherein Sudeley Castell standeth.

Campden is 6 myles northest from Winchcomb & 5 southest from Euesholme in Worcestershire.

Stow on the Would standeth on *the* est syde of Glocestershire, wthin 2 myles of Oxfordshire, 7 myles from Campden & as many from Winchcomb.

Lech, commonly called *North Lech*, standeth on the head of a small river named Lech, which falleth into the Thames at Lechlade, and is 6 myles south from Stow on *the* Wold, & as many west from Burford in Oxfordshire.

Lechlade standeth vppon *the* Thames, which there parteth Glocestershire from a corner of Barkshire, wthin half a myle of Oxfordshire & wthin a myle of Wiltshire, 8 myles southest from Northlech.

Cirncester, commonly called *Cicetur*, standeth vppon *the* river of Churn, which is *the* principallest head that the Thames hath, & springeth in Cotswold, out of Cobberley Poole, 6 myles est from Glocester. It is 8 myles directly west from Lechlade, & was in tyme past a goodly cittie, beffore Glocester was builded.

Stroud standeth on *the* south syde of Cotswold Playn vppon *the* river of Stroud which springeth in *the* said playne, & falleth into *the* Severn, 5 myles beneath Glocester, distant 8 myles west from Cicetur, & 7 southest from Glocester.

Minchin Hampton is 5 myles southest from Stroud.

Tetbury is 4 myles southest from Minchin Hampton, hard by Wiltshire.

Dursley is 6 myles west from Tetbury, and standeth on a small brook named Cam, which 4 myles thence falleth into the Seuern.

Wotton under Hedge is 3 litle¹ myles¹ directly south from Dursley. *[leaf 76]*

Wickwar is 3 myles south southest from Wotton. Betwene this towne & Wotton, lyeth a whole parish of Wiltshire called Kingswood.

Chipping-Sodbury is 3 myles southest from Wickwar.

Marsfeld standeth within a myle of Wiltshire, within 2 myles of Somersetshire, 10 myles from Bristow, in the way to London, & 5 southest from Chipping-Sodbury.

Thornbury is 9 myles northwards from Bristow, & within 2 myles of the Seuerne, where there is a fayre howse belonging to the L. Bukley.

Barkley is a proper litle towne & castell, which geueth name to the L. Barkley, and standeth 5 myles north from Thornbury, vppon a small river, within a myle of the Seuern. Now I haue named all the market townes in Gloucestershire which ly on this syde the Seuern, I will pass ouer to those 3 which lye beyond the said river.

Newnham standeth vppon the Seuern, 6 myles beneath Gloucester, on the south syde of Deane Forrest. *[leaf 76]*

Deane (comonly called *Great Deane*, for difference of *Litle Deane*, 2 myles thence), standeth on the other syde of the Forrest of Deane, whereof it taketh name, & is 4 myles northwest from Newnham, within a myle of Herefordshyre.

Newent is 4 myles north from Dean, within a myle of Herefordshire, & within 2 myles of Worcestershire.

Forrests in Gloucestershire

The Forrest of Dean reacheth from Chepstow till it come within 3 myles of Tewkesbury, which is 20 myles.

Kingswood Forrest is hard by Bristow.

Gloucestershire hath 2 parishes lying in Warwikshyre, & two in Oxfordshyre. And for the same it hath lying within it 4 peces of Worcestershyre, 2 of Wiltshyre, & one of Barkshyre.

*HEREFORDSHYRE. *[leaf 80]

[The upper part of the page contains 4 Coats of Arms — see Plate XI., Nos. 6 to 9.]

Herefordshire is in a maner round & about 24 myles ouer ech way. It hath Worcestershyre on the northest, Gloucestershyre on the southest, Monmouthshyre on the south, Brecknockshyre on the southwest, Radnorshyre on the west, & Shropshyre on the north. In which countrey besydes the cittie of Hereford) there is 7 market townes, & about 208 parish churches.

* At the top of the page is the Coat of Arms of the city of Hereford — see Plate I.] *[leaf 80]

Hereford is the cittie which geueth name to the whole countrey and standeth almost in the middest of the shyre vppon the river of Wye 21 myles from Gloucester, which river springeth at the same hill that the Seuern doth and passeth through a pece of Montgomoryshyre & a pece of Radnorshyre & after parteth Radnorshire from Brecknockshire, vntill it enter into Herefordshyre. Three myles beneath Hereford it receaveth in the river of Lug, to be described when I come to Lemster, and then toning towards the south cometh to Ross, & from thence to Monmouth, where it taketh in the river of Monmow, and so becometh a limit betwene Monmouthshire and Gloucestershire, vntill it fall into the Seuern which is 2 myles beneath Chepstow.

Webley is 8 myles northwest from Hereford. *[leaf 81]

Kineton is 6 myles west northwest from Webbley, & within a myle of Radnorshyre.

Pembridge standeth on a small river named Arro, which falleth into the Lug, a myle beneath Lemster, and is 5 myles estwards from Kineton, and 4 northwest from Webley.

Lemster is 5 myles northest from Pembridge, and standeth vppon the river of

¹ The word *litle* is spelt "lhtle," and the word *myles* is repeated in the MS.

Lug, which springeth in Radnorshire & passeth west to Prestaine, after roning through Herefordshire, cometh to Lemster, & about 12 myles southest from thence falleth into the Wy, 3 myles beneath Hereford

Bramyard is 8 myles est from Lemster, and within 3 myles of Worcestershyre, vppon a small river named Frome, which falleth into the Lug

Ledbury standeth vppon a small river named Ludden, which falleth into the Seuern over against Glocester, & is 8 myles southest from Bramyard, within 2 myles of Glocestershyre, & within 3 myles of Maluern-Hills

* *Ross* standeth on the est side of the river of Wy, 9 myles southest from Hereford, and over against it is Wilton Castell, wherof the L. Gray of Wilton taketh name

Forrests

Haywood Forrest, by Hereford
Derefold Forrest in the northwest corner of the shyre
Bringwood Chase reacheth within a myle of Ludlow, in Shropshyre

Castells

Hereford	Kilpeck	Huntington
Wigmore	Harleswas	Lenalls
Castell Frome	The Old Towne	Stepleton
Wilton	Snowdell	Croft
Penyard	Dorston	Richards Castell
Goodridge	Bredwardin	Branton-Brian
Pembridge	Clifford	Branhill

*WORCESTERSHYRE

[Five Coats of Arms at top — see Plate IX, Nos 5 to 12]

Worcestershire hath Warwikshire on the est, Glocestershire on the south, Herefordshire on the west, Shropshyre & Staffordshyre on the north. The length is, from Tewksbury in the south to Sturbridge in the north, about 25 myles; the breadth at the south end is 16 myles, but at the north end it is as broad as it is long, which is 25 myles. In which countrey (besydes the cittie of Worcester) there is 9 market townes, & about 172 parish churches, of which nomber 2 market townes & 54 parish churches do stand on the further syde of Seuerne

* [The Coat of Arms of the city of Worcester is at the top of the page — see Plate I.]

Worcester, called in Latin *Vigornia*, in British *Caerfrangon*, is an ancient cittie, standing vppon the Seuern, & almost in the middest of the shyre

Droitwich (comonly called *Durtwich*) is 5 myles northest from Worcester, & standeth vppon a small river named Salwarp, which 3 myles above Worcester falleth into the Seuern. At this towne is great store of whyte salt made

* *Beawdlean* (comonly called *Bewdley*) standeth on the west syde of Seuern, within a myle of Shropshyre, & within 2 myles of Staffordshyre, 10 myles north northwest from Worcester

Kedermister is 2 myles est northest from Bewdley, and standeth vppon the river of Stoure which 3 myles thence falleth into the Seuern

Sturbridge standeth vppon the said river of Stour, which there parteth Worcestershire from Staffordshire, 5 myles northest from Kedermister

Bromsgrove standeth on the head of the river of Salwarp beffore named, 5 myles northest from Durtwich

Eueshoim (comonly called *Evsham*) standeth vppon the river of Auon, 12 myles southest from Worcester, within 2 myles of Glocestershyre. Betwene this towne & Campden, in Glocestershire (which is 4 myles), lyeth the Vale of Euesholm, but it is most part in Glocestershyre

Pershore standeth vppon the said river of Auon, 4 myles west from Euesholme

Vpton standeth on *the* west syde of *the* Seuerne, 7 myles beneath Worcester, and 5 myles from Tewksbury, in Glocestershyre

Shipton standeth in a peece of Worcestershire, which is compassed round about *[leaf 83b]* with Warwikshire, which pece is north & south 8 myles long, but in some places not passing a myle brode, & in no place aboue 2 myles brode, wherein (beside Shipton) there is 3 parish churches, with certain villages, & gentlemens howses This towne is 10 myles est from Euesholme, & standeth vppon a small river named Stoure, which falleth into *the* Auon, a myle beneath Stretford vppon Auon

Worcestershire hath 4 other peeces lying in Glocestershyre (as beffore hath byn declard), & one pece in Staffordshyre, and it hath within it one peece of Staffordshyre, & another peece of Herefordshire

Forrests

Fecknam Forrest, on *the* est syde of Countrey, which taketh name of Fecknam hard by

Wyre Forrest, by Bewdley, is halff in Shropshyre

Maluern Hills do part Worcestershire from Herefordshyre, but are most part in Worcestershyre, taking name of Great Maluern & Litle Maluern, hard by

[leaf 84a contains Coats of Arms of Earls of Warwick see Plate VI]

WARWIKSHYRE *[leaf 84b]*

Warwickshire hath Leicestershire on *the* est, Northamptonshire on *the* southest, Oxfordshyre on *the* south, Glocestershyre on *the* southwest, Worcestershyre on *the* west, & Staffordshyre on the northwest The length from the north to *the* south is 34 myles the breadth 20 myles, in some places more, & in some less In which countrey (besydes the cittie of Couentrie) there is 12 market townes, & about 209 parish churches

[At the lower part of the page is the Cont of Arms of the town of Warwick see Plate I]

Warwick was first founded by Guitheling K of Brittains, and after, by Gwar (the *[leaf 85]* first Erle therof) named Ceergwar, & after Gwarwik It is an ancient towne & castell, standing vppon the river of Auon, which springeth in Northamtonshyre, & for *the* space of 4 myles is a limite betwene *the* same & Leecestershyre, and after entring into Warwikshyre, passeth westwards to Rugby, Wolston, Rorton, & Stonley, and then torneth sowethwest to Warwik, Stretford vppon Auon, Binton, and Bitford, and after entring through Worcestershyre, by Euesholme, & Pershore, receving sundry ryvers by *the* way, falleth into *the* Seuern at Tewksbury

[The remainder of the page is occupied with a Coat of Arms see Plate VIII, No 4]

[View of Coventry at top see Plate XXVI] *[leaf 85b]*

Couentrie is one of the bravest citties in England, and standeth in the middest of the realme, being well walled about distant 8 myles north northest from Warwick, and as many southest from Colshill Halff way betwene Couentrie & Warwik ys *the* famous castell of Kenelmwerth, or Kenelwerth, comonly called Killingworth, which belongeth to *the* Erle of Leecster

Rugby is 10 myles southest from Couentrie, & 3 north from Dunchurch, within *[leaf 86]* 2 myles of Leecestershyre, and lyke distance from Northamptonshyre

Southam is 7 myles southwest from Rugby, & as many southest from Warwik

Kineton is 7 myles southwest from Southam, & as many south from Warwick

Stretford standeth vppon *the* Auon, 7 myles southwest from Warwik, & 6 northwest from Kineton, within a myle of Glocestershyre

Aulcester standeth vppon a river named Arow, which 3 myles south from thence falleth into *the* Auon, distant 7 myles west from Stretford, & as many north from Evesholm, and within 2 myles of Worcestershyre

Henley is 5 myles northest from Aulcester, & 6 west from Warwik, vppon a small river, which falleth into *the* Arow, at Aulcester

Solihull is 7 myles north from Henley, & 8 west from Couentry.

Colshill is 5 myles north northest from Solihull, & 8 northwest from Coventrie, and standeth not far from a small river, named Col, which a myle north from thence falleth into *the* Tame, which ronneth to Tamworth

[leaf 86v] *Bremicham (comonly called Bermicham)* is a proper towne, with a high spyre steple, where great store of knyves are made, for allmost all *the* townes men are cutlers, or smithes. It standeth in *the* northwest corner of Warwikshyre, within a myle of Staffordshyre, in *the* way from Shrewsbury to London

Atherston standeth vppon *the* river of Anker which there parteth Warwikshyre from Leicestershyre, 8 myles northest from Colshill, & as many north from Couentrie, which river falleth into *the* Tame at Tamworth

Nuneaton standeth vppon *the* head of *the* said river of Anker, 3 myles south from Atherston

[leaf 87]
*LLICESTERSHYRE
[Five Coats of Arms at top — see Plate V, Nos. 12 to 16.]

Next to Warwikshyre on *the* est lyeth Leicestershire, which hath on *the* est Lincolnshyre, on *the* southest corner Rutland on *the* south Northamptonshyre on *the* west Warwikshyre, and on *the* north hath Darbyshyre & Nottinghamshire. The length thereof is from *the* est to *the* west 25 myles, and the breadth is about 20 myles. In which countrey (besydes Leicester) there is nyne market townes & 244 parish churches besydes villages, gentlemens howses, & castells

[leaf 87v] * [At the top of the page is the Coat of Arms of the city of Leicester — see Plate II.]

Leicester is an ancient cittie, standing almost in *the* middest of *the* shyre, vppon *the* river of Soure, which springeth 4 myles north of Lutterworth, keping his course northest to Leicester, Belgraue, & Cussington, where it meeteth with a great river coming from *the* est named Wreak, & then torneth northwards to Mount Sorell, & Loughborow, & 4 myles thence falleth into *the* Trent

Harborow standeth on *the* head of *the* river Welland, which there parteth Leicestershyre from Northamptonshyre, distant 12 myles south southest from Leicester

Lutterworth is 9 myles west northwest from Harborow, within a myle of Warwik- shyre, and standeth on a small river which meeteth with the Auon at Rugby

[leaf 88] *Hinckley* standeth within a myle of Warwikshyre, 8 myles northwest from Lutterworth, & 7 west southwest from Leicester

Bosworth is 4 myles northest from Hinckley, & 7 west northwest from Leicester

Ashby de la Zouch standeth within a myle of Darbyshire, 7 myles north from Bosworth

Loughborow standeth not far from *the* river of Soure, 9 myles est from Ashby de la Zouch & within a myle of Nottinghamshire

Mount-Sorell standeth on a hill not far from *the* said river, 4 myles south from Loughborow & 5 north from Leicester

Melton-Moubray standeth vppon *the* river of Wreak, 8 myles est from Mount Sorell, within 3 myles of Rutland

Waltham on the Would is 3 myles northest from Melton, & within 4 myles of Lincolnshyre

Forrests

Leicester Forrest by Leicester, on *the* west syde
Charnwood Forrest, west of Mount Sorell

[leaf 88v]
*RUTLAND
[Coat of Arms of Earls of Rutland at the top — see Plate XVI, Nos. 8 to 10.]

Rutland ys *the* least shyre in England. It is 3 cornerd & every corner is 10 myles. On the west it hath Leicestershyre, on *the* northest Lincolnshire, & on *the* southest Northamptonshyre, from the which it is devyded by the river of Welland. In which countrey I ffynd to be 2 market townes, and 48 parish churches

Okeham ys the shyre towne of Rutland, and standeth on the west syde of the countrey, within 3 myles of Lecestershyre, and on the est syde therof lyeth the Vale of Catmouse

Vppingham ys 5 myles south from Okeham, within 3 myles of Lecestershyre, & as nigh to Northamptonshyre

Forrest

Lyfeld Forrest lyeth betwene Okeham & Vppingham

[leaf 89b contains Coats of Arms of Earls of Lincoln see Plate IX]

*LINCOLNSHIRE

Lincolnshire is one of the greatest shyres in England, and contayneth in length, ffrom Stamford in the south vnto the river of Humber, over against Hull, 55 myles. The breadth in the middest is 32 myles, on the southend it is 28 myles brode, and on the north end 20. On the est syde it is environed with the mean sea, on the south it toucheth vppon Norfolk, Cambridgeshyre, Northamptonshyre, Rutland & Leicestershyre, on the northwest & north Yorkshyre. It is devyded into 3 partes, namely, Lindsey, Kesteuen, & Holland. In Lindsey (besydes the cittie of Lincolne) there is 16 market townes, & 354 parish churches. In Kesteuen are 7 market townes & 155 parish churches. In Holland are 5 market townes & 33 parish churches. So that there is in all 28 market townes and 542 parish churches. Which market townes I will name in order as they do ly, & with every province apart, begining first with the province of Lindsey

*[The Coat of Arms of the city of Lincoln is at the upper part of the page see Plate II]

Lincolne is one of the greatest citties in England, and standeth in the prouince of Lindsey, vppon the river Witham, which springeth within a myle of Rutland, at South Witham, & so passeth to North Witham, Grantham, Beckingham, & Lincolne, and here it devydeth Lindsey from Kesteuen, ffrom whence there [is] a dych digged to the Trent, called Fosdich, about 8 myles long, ffrom Lincoln it kepeth his course estwards to Tatershall, where it receaveth in a river named Banc, and then passeth through the Fennes to Boston, and about 4 myles thence falleth into the sea

Ganesborow standeth vppon the river of Trent, which in that place parteth Lincolnshire from Nottinghamshyre, about 12 myles northwest from Lincolne

Market-Rasin standeth in the middest of Lindsey, about 14 myles est from Ganesborow, 10 northest from Lincolne, and vppon the head of the river of Ankolm, or Ankam, which roning from thence to Newsted, Glandford-Bridge, & Horstow, falleth into the Humber

Castor is 6 myles north from Market Rasin

Kirton, in Lindsey, is 8 myles west from Castor, and as many northest from Ganesborow

Glandford-Bridge standeth vppon the Ankam, 6 myles northest from Kirton, & as many northwest from Castor

Burton standeth vppon the Trent, 7 myles northwest from Glandford Bridge, & within 3 myles of the Humber. Over against Burton is the Isle of Axholme, which is 10 myles[1] & 5 brode, and belongeth all to Lincolneshyre

Limberg (comonly called *Great Limberg*, for diffrence of *Litle Limberg* hard by), is 8 myles south southest from Barton, & 6 est from Glandford Bridge

Barton standeth vppon the Humber, almost right against Hull, 8 myles northest from Barton, & 2 est from the mouth of the Ankolm

Grimsby standeth on the Humber syde over against the Spurnhead, 7 myles est from Limberg

Saltflete standeth on the sea syde, 10 myles southest from Grimsby

Loweth is 6 myles southwest from Saltfleet

---
[1] Thus in the MS

Alford is 9 myles southest from Louth, & 5 from the sea

Wainflete is 8 myles south southest from Alford, and standeth in the est Fenn, 3 myles from the sea

Spilsby is 6 myles westward from Wainfleet, and within 3 myles of Bollinbrok Castell

Horncastle standeth vppon a small river named Bane, which falleth into the Witham beneath Tatershall, & is 7 myles westwards from Spilsby

Tatershall standeth vppon the said river, which a myle from thence falleth into the Witham, and is 6 myles south from Horncastell

Now I have named all the townes in Lindsey, I will proceed with them in Kesteuen, which is in the south part of Lincolnshyre

[leaf 92]

*Buckingham standeth vppon the river of Witham, 10 myles southwards from Lincolne

Grantham standeth also vppon the said river, 20 myles directly south from Lincolne, and hath a high spyre steple, which (now Paules Steple is downe) is counted for the highest steple in England

Sleford is 10 myles northest from Grantham, & lyke distance from Tatershall, halff way betwene both

Fokingham is 6 myles south from Sleford, & 8 est from Grantham

Borne is 8 myles south from Fokingham

Market-Deping is 5 myles south from Borne, 5 west from Crowland, & 5 est from Stamford, and standeth vppon the river of Welland, which there parteth Lincolnshire from Northamptonshire

Stamford, a brave walled towne, great & ancient, standeth vppon the said river of Welland, 5 myles west from Market-Deping, hard vppon Rutland, & part of the towne standeth in Northamptonshyre

Now remayneth the 5 market townes in Holland, whose names do follow

*[leaf 92b]

*Boston, a walled towne, standeth vppon the river of Witham, 9 myles from Tatershall, and 4 myles the sea,[1] and is one of the principallest townes in Lincolnshyre

Dunnington is 2 myles southwest from Boston, 7 estwards from Fokingham, & as many from the Washes, which ly betwene Lincolnshyre & Norfolk

Spalding standeth vppon the river of Welland, 7 myles south from Dunnington, & within 4 myles of the Washes

Quaplode standeth vppon a salt creek, 4 myles est northest from Spalding, & 2 from the Washes

Crowland is 7 myles south from Spalding, 5 est from Market-Deping, and standeth not far from the river of Welland, which there parteth it selff into two partes, over the which is a wunderfull stone bridge, of one only arch

[leaf 93]

*NOTTINGHAMSHYRE

[Coats of Arms of Erlls of Nottingham at top — see Plate XVI]

Nottinghamshire hath Lincolnshyre on the est, Leicestershyre on the south, Darbyshyre on the west, and Yorkshyre on the north. The length therof is from the north to the south 35 myles, the breadth in the middest is 20 myles, but at ech end it is somwhat narrower. In it are 9 market townes, and 200 parish churches, of which nomber 72 do stand on this syde the Trent

[leaf 93b]

* [At the top of the page is the Coat of Arms of the town of Nottingham — see Plate II]

Nottingham is a brave towne & castell, standing vppon a small river named Lyne, which not far of falleth into the Trent, distant 10 myles est from Darby, & 12 southwest from Newark vppon Trent

Mannsfeld standeth on the west syde of the shyre within 3 myles of Darbyshyre, & 12 from Nottingham

[1] Thus in the MS

Warsop standeth also within 2 myles of Darbyshyre, & 4 myles north from *[leaf 94]
Maunsfeld

Worksopp standeth also within 3 myles of Darbyshyre, & lyke distance from Yorkshyre, 4 myles north from Warsop

Blith is 4 myles north from Worksop, & 3 south from Beautree in Yorkshyre

Retford standeth uppon a small river named Iddle, which ronneth from thence to Beautree in Yorkshyre, & after meeteth with a peece of the Trent, & maketh the Isle of Axholme. It is 4 myles southest from Blith

Litlbur gh standeth uppon the Trent, which there parteth Nottinghamshyre from Lincolnshyre, 5 myles est from Retford, & as many south from Ganesborow in Lincolnshire

Newark standeth on the est syde of the Trent, 14 myles south from Litleburg, & 4 from Beckingham in Lincolnshyre

Suthwell is 5 myles west from Newark, & 9 northest from Nottingham

The Forrest of Sherwood lyeth in the middest of Nottinghamshyre

[leaf 94b contains Coats of Arms of Earls of Derby see Plate XIV]

DARBYSHIRE *[leaf 95]

Darbishire hath Nottinghamshyre on the est, Leicestershire on the southest, Staffordshire and Cheshire on the west, and Yorkshyre on the north. The length therof, from the north to the south, is 40 myles on the north end. It is nere 30 myles brode, in the middest 15, and at the south end (especially that part which lyeth south of the Trent) not passing 6 myles brode. In which countrey I fynd to be 8 market townes, & about 159 parish churches besydes villages, gentlemens howses, & castells. Of which parish churches, 18 are on the south of Trent

Darby is a proper towne, with 5 parish churches in it, but is not walled, nor hath *[leaf 95]
any castell, and standeth on the southest of the shyre, 10 myles west from Nottingham, uppon the river of Darwen, which springeth in the north part of the said countrey, not farr from the wood head in the Peak Hills, and kepeth his course southest to Newchapell, Dawenchapell, Padley, & Rousley, where it taketh in a river named Wy, which cometh from Buxton Well, & so passeth to Darley. Darley Hall, Matlock, Wistanwelbridge, & two myles thence taketh in a river on the est syde named Amber, and at Dunsfeld another, of the west syde, named Ecclesborne, and the third at Darby, fitom whence, 6 myles of, it falleth into the Trent

Ashborne standeth on the west syde of the shyre, uppon a litle brooke, which a myle thence falleth into the Doue, which river of Doue parteth Darbyshyre from Staffordshyre all his course, which is from Maxfeld Forrest till it fall into the Trent, which is 3 myles beneath Burton. This towne is 8 myles northwest from Darby

Wirksworth is 5 myles northest from Ashborne and standeth on the head of a *[leaf 96]
small river named Ecclesborne, which falleth into the Darwen at Dunsfeld

Bankwell (comonly called *Bakewell*) standeth in the Peak, uppon the river Wy, 8 myles northwest from Wirksworth

Tuddeswall (comonly called *Tisdale*) standeth also in the Peak, 5 myles northwest from Bakewell

The *Chapell in the Frith* (comonly called *Chapell Frith*) standeth also in the Peak, 5 myles northwest from Tisdale, uppon the head of a small river named Firth, which 3 myles from thence falleth into the Goit, which river of Goit parteth Darbyshyre from Cheshyre all his course

Chesterfeld is the greatest towne in Darbyshyre next to Darby and standeth uppon the river of Rother, which falleth into the Don at Rotheram in Yorkshyre, and is distant 16 myles directly, 8 south fiom Sheatfeld, in Yorkshyre, & as[1] northwest from Maunsfeld, in Nottinghamshyre

Alfreton is 7 myles south from Chesterfeld, 10 north from Darby, & 3 northwest from Codnor Castell, and standeth uppon the river of Amber

[1] Thus in MS

6

[leaf 96b]

*_Forrests_

Peak Forrest, the only forrest in Darbyshyre

Castells

Melborn	Chatsworth, a goodly pallace	Codnor
Graisley	belonging to the Countess	Winfield Manor
Castel in the Peak	of Shrewsbury	Boulsouer
		Horeston

[leaf 97]

*STAFFORDSHYRE

[Two Coats of Arms at top — see Plate XIII, Nos. 3 and 4.]

Staffordshire hath Darbyshyre on the northest, Warwikshyre on the southest, Worcestershire on the south, Shropshyre on the southwest, & Cheshire on the northwest. The length therof is, from the Douehead in the north to Areley vppon Seuern in the south[1] about 42 myles. The breadth in the middest is 25 myles, but at both endes it is sharpe lyke a mill pick. In which countrey (besydes Lichfeld) there is 12 market townes, 150 parish churches, & 26 chapells which may pass for parish churches, so that there is in all 176, besides villages, gentlemens howses, and castells

[leaf 97b]

*[View of Stafford at top — see Plate XXVI.]

Stafford is a proper litle towne, walled about, standing in the middest of the shyre, vppon the river of Sow, which falleth into the Trent 3 myles est from thence. The castell standeth almost a myle from the towne.

[View of Lichfeld in centre of the page — see Plate XXVI.]

Lichfeld is a great cittie, and an ancient bishopps seat, standing 12 myles southest from Stafford, but vnwalled, all saving the minster, which minster was founded by King John

[leaf 98]

*Tamworth is 5 myles southest from Lichfeld, and standeth at the confluence of 2 rivers, Tame, & Anker, which fyve myles north from thence do fall into the Trent. The Castell & halff the towne standeth in Warwikshyre

Walshall (comonly called Wasall) standeth on a hill, at the head of the said river of Tame, 9 myles west southwest from Tamworth, 6 southwest from Lichfeld, & as many northwest from Bermicham

Wulverhampton standeth also vppon a hill, 5 myles westwards from Walshall

Brewood is 5 myles north northwest from Wullerhampton, & 6 directly south from Stafford

Eccleshall is 6 myles northwest from Stafford, and hath a castell belonging to the Bishopp of Lichfeld

Stone standeth on the Trent, 3 myles northest from Eccleshall, and in the way from Chester to London

New-castell (called Newcastell vnder Lyne) is 6 myles northwest from Stone, & within 4 myles of Cheshyre

Leeke standeth on the northend of the shyre, amongst the hilles, 8 myles northest from Newcastell, & as many est from Congleton, in Cheshire, vppon a river named Chunnet, which 10 myles southest from thence falleth into the Doue. A myle north from Leek, on the said river was Delacress Abbay

[leaf 98b]

*Vttoxiter (comonly called Vtter), standeth not farr from the Doue (which parteth Staffordshyre from Darbyshyre) 10 myles est from Stone. Betwene this towne & Stone is Chartley Castell

Pagets-Bramley is 4 myles south from Vteeter, and standeth not far from the river of Blith, which 5 myles southest from thence falleth into the Trent

Burton standeth vppon the Trent, which there parteth Staffordshyre from Darbyshyre, 8 myles est from Pagets Bramley, & as many northest from Lichfeld

[1] "north" corrected into "south" by a different hand

Staffordshyre hath 2 parishes lying together in Worcestershyre, and Worcestershyre hath one parish in Staffordshire, which is Dudley. But Dudley Castell & park also is in Stafford-shyre

Forrests

Cankwood lyeth betwene Stafford & Lichfeld
Pensnet Chase, on the south end by Dudley Castell
Needwood Forrest, on the est syde, by Burton

Castells

Stafford	Chartley
Eccleshall	Tetbury —— Tetbury is now made a market towne also
Healy	Dudley
Alton	Sturton

*SHROPSHYRE *[leaf 99]

[Two Coats of Arms at top see Plate XI, Nos 15 and 16]

Shropshire taketh name of Shrewsbury, standing vppon the Seuern, which ronneth through the shyre so equally that it is hard to judge whether syde is greater. It hath Staffordshyre on the est, Worcestershyre on the southest, Herefordshyre on the south, Radnorshyre on the southwest, Montgomoryshire on the west, Denbighshyre on the northwest, Cheshire, & peece of Flintshyre on the north. The length from the north to the south is 32 myles, the breadth 20, in some places more, & in some less. On the north syde of Seuerne is 8 market townes & 86 parish churches, on the south syde there is 4 market townes & 120 parish churches, which maketh in all 206 parish churches, whereunto may be added 20 chapells, so that the totall some is 226, besydes villages, wherwith it is well stored, gentlemens howses, & castells

* [At the top of the page is the Coat of Arms of the town of Shrewsbury see Plate II] *[leaf 99b]

Shrewsbury is a brave towne walled about, & almost enuironed with the Seuerne, over the which it hath 2 ffayre stone bridges, and standeth in the very middest of the shyre. The Brittains or Walshmen call it in their language Ymwthig, that is to say, a place where willows do grow. In Latin it is called Salopia, which seemeth to come from the Latin word Salix, a willow

*Oswalds-tre (comonly called Oswestre) a walled towne, is 12 myles northwest *[leaf 100] from Shrewsbury, and within 2 myles of Denbighshire

Wem is xi myles est northest from Oswestree, and 7 ffrom Shrewsbury, and standeth vppon a small river named Roddon, which ronneth from thence to Morton Corbet Castell, & lastly falleth into the Terne

Prees is 3 myles north from Wem, and hard by it is a great heath, called Prees Heath

Whitchurch is 5 myles north northwest from Prees, and standeth on the northend of the shyre, within two myles of Cheshyre, & within one myle of a parcell of Flintshire, on the north syde of a litle brook, which cometh out of Blakmer Mere, and falleth into the Dee

Drayton standeth vppon the river of Terne, which there parteth Shropshyre from Staffordshyre, 8 myles from Whitchurch

Newport toucheth also vppon Staffordshyre, & is 7 myles southest from Drayton

Wellington is a great towne standing 5 myles south southwest from Newport, and about 7 myles estwards from Shrewsbury

*Wenlock is 5 myles south from Wellington, and two myles south from the *[leaf 100b] Seuern

Bridge-North standeth vppon the Seuern, 5 myles southest from Wenlock, and is a proper walled towne with a castell, & two churches in the towne, as I heare

Ludlow, a proper walled towne, is the place where the Courtes for Wales are kept, & the Marches of the same, and standeth on the southend of the shyre 13 myles south southwest from Bridge North, & within two myles of Herefordshyre, where the river of Corue falleth into the Temd, which river of Temd, at the head, parteth Shropshyre from Radnorshyre, and entring into a corner of Herefordshyre receaveth the river of Clun, & after, in Shropshyre, the river of Onny, 2 myles above Ludlow, ffrom Ludlow it ronneth through Worcestershyre, receving dyvers small ryvers by the way, falleth into the Seuerne, 2 myles beneath Worcester

Bishoppscastle is 10 myles west northwest from Ludlow, & 5 southest from Montgomory

These 4 townes last recyted do stand on the south syde of the Seuerne, the rest do stand on the north syde

[leaf 101]

*Forrests

Morf Forrest, by Bridge Morph, or Bridge North
Babins Wood Forrest, ⎫
Condigate Forrest,   ⎬ by Oswestree
Treuelegh Forrest,   ⎭
Hockstow Forrest, betwene Shrewsbury & Montgomory
Clun Forrest, on the southwest corner of the shyre
Mocktree Forrest, by Ludlow
Wyre Forrest, by Bewdley, is halff in Worcestershire
Shorlet Wood, by Wenlock
Kings Wood, by Newport, & dyvers other lesser

Castells

Shrewsbury	Wattelsburg	Corsham
Bridge-north	Caus	Shipton
Morton-Corbet	Powderbach	Hopton
Whittenton	Atton-Bunnell	The New Castle
Knokin	Charlton	Redcastle
Shrawardon	Howgate	Clun Castell
Rowton	Brancroft	Tong Castell

[leaf 101b contains 8 Coats of Arms see Plate VIII, Nos 5 to 12]

[f. 102]

*CHESHYRE

Cheshire taketh name of the cittie of Chester, and hath Darbyshyre on the est, Staffordshyre on the southest, Shropshyre & a parcell of Flintshyre on the south, Denbighshyre & the rest of Flintshire on the west. On the northwest it hath the Irish-Sea, on the north Lancashyre, from the which it is devyded by the river of Marsey, and toucheth on the northest corner uppon Yorkshyre. The longest length is from the wood head (where the river of Marsey springeth) to the furthest part of Werall (where it falleth into the sea) 44 myles; the brodest place is from Titley Hall in the south to Crosfordbridge in the north, about 25 myles; the compass round about 112 myles. In which countrey (besydes the cittie of Chester) there is 11 market townes, & 87 parish churches, & 34 churches which beare the name of chapells, which is in all 121. To these if you add 9 parish churches that are within Chester then is the number just 130; besydes villages, gentlemens howses, & castells

[The remainder of the page is occupied with a View of Chester see Plate XXIV]

[f. 102 b]

Chester is a most ancient & famous cittie, standing uppon the river of Dee, which is there about 200 foote brode, over the which there is a fayre stone bridge of 8 arches. The castell standeth on a hyll within the walles, which walles are in compass round about 2000 paces, which is two myles, and hath 4 principall gates, with very fayre & large suburbes. The barres of the citties are of stone. Within the liberties of the cittie are 9 parish churches, besydes chapells & other religious places. The howses are builded in such sort, that a man may go from one place of the cittie to another and never come into the streetes, which manner of building I have not hard of in any other place of Christendome. The said river of Dee springeth in Merinothshyre, & passeth through a lake called Lhin Tegill, after (receiving dyvers rivers by the way) it entreth through Denbighshyre, where (so soone as it hath receved the river of Keriog) it parteth Shropshyre from Denbighshyre, & after hath Flintshire on the right syde & Denbighshyre on the lefit, vntill it come almost to Shocklidge, where it parteth Cheshire from Denbighshyre, vntill it come 2 myles beneath Holt Castell, and then for the space of a myle parteth Flintshire from Cheshire, & after hath Cheshyre on both sydes, lastly it toucheth on the south syde of the cittie of Chester, where (after it hath passed the bridge) it fetcheth a round compasse, making a fayre playne called The Rood Eie, toucheth also on the west syde of the cittie. And after it is past the New Tower of the said cittie, it becommeth alwaies broder and broder, vntill it fall into the sea, which is 16 myles from Chester.

*Nantewh, called in Latin, Vicus Malbanus) is accompted the greatest towne in *[leaf 10, Cheshyre next to Chester, and standeth 14 myles southest from Chester, vppon the river of Weever, in the way to London, where great store of whyte salt is made. It hath one bryne pitt, from the which the wichwallers do carry their bryne to the wich-howses, where they seeth it in caulderns of lead, & so make salt. The said river of Weever springeth out of Ridley Poole (which poole reacheth from Ridley to Cholmley, in length two myles), and kepeth his course southest to Wrenbury, where it taketh in a small brooke that cometh out of Marbury Mere, & beneath Sandford Bridge another that cometh out of Combermere and not farr from Aulem, the third, that cometh from Morton Say in Shropshyre, and then kepeth his course northwards, through the Nantwich, Minshull, Weever, the Vale Roiall, and at Northwich meeteth with the Dane, & halffe a myle beneath the towne, with the Peeuer, and then torneth northwest to Weuerham or Wercham, Acton Bridge, Frodsham Bridge, & a myle from thence meeteth with the Marsey, where it loseth name.

Malpas, called in Latin Malus-pissus, is a proper towne, with 2 churches, standing on a hyll southwest from Chester. It hath market every Sonday, and therfore some do not accompt it for a market towne.

*Northwich standeth whereas the 2 rivers of Weuer & Dane do meet 10 myles *[leaf 103^] directly north from Nantwich. Here is also a salt pitt, from the which they draw bryne which ronneth on the ground in woodden troughs to the wich howses.

Knutsford is 5 myles northest from Northwich. There is two townes with 2 churches hard together, called Higher Knutsford & Lower Knutsford; they have both ffayres, & one of them every week a market.

Altrincham is 5 myles directly north from Knutsford, on the north syde of Cheshyre, 3 miles from Crosford Bridge.

Stopford is 6 myles est northest from Altrincham, and standeth vppon the river of Marsey, which springeth at the wood head, in the confynes of Yorkshyre, and parteth Cheshyre from Darbishire, vntill it meet with the Goit, and then crosseth through a corner of Cheshyre, meeteth above Stopford with the Taume, which parteth Cheshire from Lancashire, till it meeteth with the Marsey. From Stopford the Marsey kepeth his course westwards (all his way parting Cheshyre from Lancashyre) to Chedley, Northen, Ashton on Marsey bank, & beneath Crosford Bridge, at Flixton, taketh in the Irwell, that cometh from Manchester & at Rixton the Bollin that cometh from Maxfeld, & so goeth to Warrington, Runckorn, & Weston, where it meeteth with the Weeuer, which maketh it a myle brode at a full sea, but at Lirpole it is not halff so brode. Three myles from Lirpoole, it falleth into the sea, making a fayre haven called Lirpoole Hauen.

*Maxfeld is a fayre towne, with a high spyre steple, standing 8 myles south from *[leaf 104 Stopford, vppon the head of the river of Bullin, which springeth in Maxfeld Forest, hard by, and ronneth from Maxfeld to Prestbury (the greatest parish in all Cheshyre), Newton Chapell, Wimslow, Pownall, Ringay, Ashley, Bowden, & Dunham, and not farr from Warburton, falleth into the Marsey, at Rixton.

Conghton is six myles south southwest from Maxfeld, and standeth vppon the river of Dane, which springeth in Maxfeld Forrest, and parteth Cheshyre from Staffordshyre, till it come within a myle of Congleton. From Congleton it passeth to Damport, Hulms Chapel, & Croxton where it taketh in the river of Wheelock, & so passeth to Shipbroke by Dancham, & at Northwich falleth into the Weever

Midlewich, so called, because it standeth betwene the other two wiches, is a great towne, but yet no market towne, although it have a litle market every Saterday. Yet it hath yearly two fayres, and hath 2 salt pitts, where they make salt

Sandbach, standeth on the high bank of the small river of Wheelock, 4 myles southest from Midlewich, and was of late yeares made a market towne by Sir Joh Radcliff, who is owner therof

Tarvin is 4 myles est from Chester, and was of late yeares also made a market towne, by Sir John Sauage, vnto whom it belongeth

*[leaf 104*b*]* *Frodsham* towne & castell standeth 8 myles northest from Chester, & was of late yeares made a market towne by Sir John Sauage

Haulton towne & castell is 2 miles northest from Frodsham, which was in tymes past a market towne, and hath yet Burgeses & other priveleges as a towne corporat

Forrests

| Delamere Forrest | | Maxfeld Forrest |

Castells

| Chester | Frodsham | Beeston | Oldcastle |
| Shotwik | Dunham | Halton | |

[leaf 105*a* contains Coat of Arms of the Duchy of Lancaster see Plate I]

*[leaf 105*b*]*

LANCASHYRE

Lancashire lyeth along the Irish Sea, reaching fīrom Cheshyre to Cumberland. On the est it hath Yorkshyre, on the south Cheshyre, on the west the said Irish Sea, on the north it toucheth vppon Cumberland & Westmerland. The length therof is from the north to the south 55 myles, the breadth at the southend is 36 myles, but the more northward it goeth, the narrower it is, so that towards the further[1] a litle beyond Lancaster (at Kent Sand, where the river of Ken falleth into the sea), the sea hath eaten through Lancashyre, & at a full sea toucheth vppon Westmerland. In this countrey I fynd to be 16 market townes and 98 parish churches and 36 chapells which may pass for churches, besydes villages, castells, and gentlemens howses, wherewithall it is very well furnished

[leaf 106] [At the top of the page is the Coat of Arms of the town of Lancaster see Plate II]

Lancaster is an old towne & castell, standing vppon the south syde of theriver Lan, which springeth in Mallerstang Forrest in Westmerland, & kepeth his course south to Kirkby Lansdale, & not farr of entreth into Lancashire by Thurland Castell, Aughton Caton, Halton & Lancaster, & about 5 myles from Lancaster it falleth into the sea

*[leaf 106*b*]* *Garstang* is 9 myles south from Lancaster, & standeth by Pillin-Moss, vppon a small river named Wyre, which springeth in Wiresdale Forrest not far from Wiresdale towne, ronneth from thence to Shyreshead, Garstang, & at Michaell Church taketh in dyvers other small rivers, and lastly falleth into Bergrode & so into the sea hard by

Kirkham standeth not far from Marton Moss, 7 myles south from Garstang, & not far from the mouth of the Ribbell

Preston comonly called *Preston in Amdernes*, is 6 myles est from Kirkham, and standeth vppon the river of Ribbell, which springeth in Yorkshyre, & crosseth through the middest of Lancashyre, into the sea

Blackborn is 7 myles est from Preston

Colne is 12 myles northest from Blackborn, & within 3 myles of Yorkshyre

[1] Thus in MS

Rochdale (comonly called *Ratchdale*) is 12 myles south from Colne, and standeth on a small river named Roch, which 5 myles thence falleth into *the* Erwell

Bury is 4 myles southwest from Rochdale, & standeth uppon the river of Irwell

Bolton is 4 myles southwest from Bury, and standeth on a small brook, which *[leaf 107]* 4 myles thence falleth into *the* Irwell

Wigan is 7 myles southwest from Bolton, & standeth uppon *the* head of *the* river Dowles, which falleth into *the* mouth of the Ribble

Ormeskirk is 8 myles west from Wigan, & within 4 myles of *the* sea Three litle myles northest from Ormeskirk is *the* goodly manor place of Lathom, belonging to *the* Erle of Darby

Lirpoole standeth within 3 myles of *the* sea, uppon *the* river of Marsey, about 9 myles south from Ormeskirk

Warrington standeth also uppon *the* Marsey, which parteth Lancashyre from Cheshyre, 12 myles south southest from Wigan

Manchester is 6 myles south from Bury, 7 ffrom Rochdale 7 from Bolton, & 5 from Stopford, in Cheshyre It is the cheiffest towne in Lancashire, next to Lancaster, & in many respects passeth *the* same, and standeth on the southest corner of *the* countrey, uppon the river of Irwell, which 6 myles from thence ffalleth into the Marsey at Flixton

Vluerston standeth in *the* furthest end of Lancashyre, nere Fournes Fells, within *[leaf 107/]* 2 myles of Leuen Sands

Daulton towne & castell is 4 myles southwest from Vluerston, & within 3 myles of Cumberland

Forrests

Bowland Forrest, part of it lyeth in Yorkshyre
Simons Wood Forrest
Wiersdale Forrest

Castells

Lancaster	Grenno	Daulton
Lathom	Hornby	Glasston
Lirpoole	Thurland	The Pyle of Foudray
Clithero	Vluerston	

[leaf 108*a* contains Coat of Arms of Yorkshire see Plate II]

*YORKSHYRE   *[leaf 108*b*]

Yorkshire ys the greatest shyre in all England, & almost as bigg as all Wales It is 4 square the length from *the* est to *the* west is 70 myles, & *the* breadth is 60 It hath on *the* west Lancashyre, on *the* northwest corner Westmerland, on the north the Bishopprik of Durham, from *the* which it is devyded by *the* river of Teese, on *the* est it hath the sea, & on the south it toucheth uppon Lincolnshire, Nottinghamshire, Darbyshyre, & Cheshyre Besydes the cittie of York, it hath 45 market townes, above 30 castells, 621 parish churches, 44 chapells, and more then 700 villages, besydes gentlemens howses But this is to be understood, that I reakon Richmondshire withall, as it is comonly so taken Howbeit Richmondshyre is (or ought to be) a shyre of it selffe, for in spirituall matters it is under the Bishopp of Chester, & not under the Archbishopp of York which shyre is about the fyft part of Yorkshyre

[leaves 109*b* and 110*a* contain nothing but 2 Coats of Arms see Plate II —leaf 110*b* is vacant]

York is *the* greatest cittie in all England, next to London, which for greatnes *[leaf 111]* & scituation (as some wryte) may be compared to Rome as I have hird Winchester compared for scituation to Jerusalem It hath 2 castells, 30 parish churches, and standeth on ech syde of *the* river of Ouse, which more properly ought to be called Eur, or Your, and therof did York first take name, as Eurwik, or Yourwik, now short York, which river of Youre springeth amonge the hills on *the* west syde of Yorkshyre, and ronneth to Midleham, Massam Rippon & beneath Borowbrigge taketh in the Swale, which cometh from Richmond & shortly after meeteth with a litle brook named Ouse, where it loses name & is called Ouse, and so passeth through York, receiving by the way the Nid, which cometh from Knaresborow & beneath York the Warf, then the Darwen and lastly the Aer, meeteth with the Trent, & is called Humber, as in the beginning of the booke hath byn declared.

Selby standeth on the west syde of the Ouse, 9 myles south from York.

Snath is 5 myles south from Selby, and standeth vppon the Aer, which 5 myles thence falleth into the Ouse.

Doncaster is 10 myles south from Snath, and standeth vppon the river of Don, which springeth not far from the wood head, & ronneth to Sheaffeld, Rotheram, & Doncaster. Lastly it parteth it selfe into two, whereof one part falleth into the Aer, and the other into Trent.

Beautre is 6 myles southest from Doncaster, & standeth vppon the river Iddle, which there parteth Yorkshire from Nottinghamshire.

Rotheram standeth whereas the river of Rother falleth into the Don, 9 myles west from Beautre, & 7 southwest from Doncaster.

Sheaffeld standeth vppon the said river of Don, 5 myles southwest from Rotheram, & within 4 myles of Darbyshire.

Barnsley is 9 myles north from Sheaffeld, & standeth vppon a small river, which falleth into the Don, not far from Doncaster.

Pontfret (comonly called *Pountfret*) is 9 myles northest from Barnesley, within 2 myles of the Aer.

Sherborne is 5 myles north from Pontfret, and standeth on a small brook which falleth into the Ouse.

Wakefeld standeth vppon the river of Calder, which 5 myles thence falleth into the Aer, and hath Pountfret on the est, Leeds on the north, & Barnsley on the south, lyke distance of 6 myles.

Leeds standeth vppon the river Aer, which springeth out of a poole called Malwater terne, & ronneth southest to Gargrave Christall Leedes, & at Castleforth taketh in the Calder, & then ronneth to Brotherton & Snath, & so into the Ouse.

Halifax is xj myles southwest from Leedes, & 12 west from Wakefeld. It standeth on a small brooke, which 2 myles thence falleth into the Calder.

Bradforth is 6 myles northest from Halifax, & as much west from Leeds, and standeth vppon a small brooke, which 2 myles thence falleth into the Aer.

Otley standeth vppon the river of Warf, which springeth not far from the place where the Ribbell springeth, nere Camhill & so ronneth to Brunsall, Addingham, Otley, Wetherby, Tadcaster & lastly falleth into the Ouse.

Wetherby standeth vppon the said river of Warf, 9 myles est from Otley, & 7 from York.

Knaresborow is 5 myles northwest from Wetherby, and standeth vppon the Nid, which springeth at Warnside Hill, and passeth to Midlesmore, Ripley Knaresborow, & lastly falleth into the Ouse.

Ripley standeth vppon the said river of Nid, 4 myles west northwest from Knaresborow.

Skipton is 13 myles southwest from Ripley, xj west from Otley, & within a myle of the Aer.

Seth standeth vppon the Ribble, 10 myles west northwest from Skipton, within 6 myles of Lancashyre.

Borowbrigg standeth vppon the Youre, 12 myles northwest from York.

Rippon standeth vppon the said river (or not far from it), 5 myles west northwest from Borowbrigg.

Massam standeth in Richmondshyre, vppon the said river of Youre, 7 myles northwest from Rippon.

Midleham standeth also in Richmondshyre, & vppon the said river, 5 myles northwest from Massam. Three myles northwest from Midlam, is Bolton Castell, belonging to the Lord Scrope.

Bedall standeth also in Richmondshyre, 7 myles northest from Midlam, vppon a small river, which falleth into the Swale.

Now cometh Richmond next to hand to be spoken of, which shall follow, with the armes of the Erles thereof

[leaf 113r contains five Coats of Arms—see Plate XVI., Nos. 11 to 15.]

*Richmond is a proper towne, with 3 parishe churches therein, and is walled about, [leaf 113v] saving on the south syde, where it hath the river of Swale, which river springeth not farr from the place where the Youre springeth, to say, at the foote of Huseatmormill Hill (which hill is a limit to Yorkshire, Richmondshyre, & Westmerland), and so ronneth to Richmond, & taking in dyvers rivers by the way, cometh to Topcliff, lastly falleth into the Youre, beneath Borowbrigg.

Alverton (comonly called *Northalerton*) is 10 myles est southest from Richmond, & in the way from York to Barwik.

Thrusk is 7 myles south southest from Northalerton, & standeth vppon a small river named Codbeck, which 3 myles thence falleth into the Swale. Three myles north from Thrusk is Vpsall Castell, wherof the L. Scrope of Vpsall taketh name.

Yarum standeth vppon the river of Teese (which parteth Yorkshire from the Bishopprick of Durham), 10 myles northest from Northalerton, and about 8 ffrom the sea.

*Stokesby is 5 myles est from Yarum, vppon a small river which falleth into the [leaf 114] Teese, a myle beneath Yarum.

Gisborow is 5 myles northest from Stokesley, vppon a small river, which 5 myles thence falleth into the sea. At the Priory of Gisborow, Wm Nevill, L. Faconbridge & Erle of Kent, is buried.

Whitby is in Cleueland, on the sea syde, on the mouth of a small river, 16 myles est from Gisborow.

Skarborow standeth also on the sea syde, xj myles south southest from Whitby.

Pickering standeth into the meane land, 13 myles west southwest from Skarborow.

Kirkby-Moresyde is 5 myles west from Pickering.

Helmesley is 4 myles southwest from Kirkby-Moresyde.

Hovingham is 4 myles southest from Helmesley.

New-Malton (so called for diffrence of *Old Malton* hard by) is 7 myles est southest from Hovingham, and standeth vppon the river of Darwen, which springeth in Blakay More & ronneth south to Hacknes, Ayton, & Garton, where it torneth towards the west to Yeddington, and there torneth south agayne to Old-Malton, New-Malton, Kirkham, Sutton on Darwen, Wresill Castell, and lastly falleth into the Ouse.

*Bridlington standeth within a myle of the sea, vppon a small river, xj myles on [leaf 114v] this syde Scarborow, & 4 myles from Flamborow Head.

Killam standeth into the land, 6 myles southwest from Bridlington, at the very head spring of the river of Hull.

Pocklington is hard by Yorkswold, vppon the head of a small river which falleth into the Darwen, & is 10 myles est from York.

Howden is 10 myles south from Pocklington, within a myle of the Ouse.

Wighton is not farr from Yorkswold, 5 myles southest from Pocklington, vppon the head of a small river called Foulney, which falleth into the Humber in 2 places over against the mouth of the Trent.

Beuerlay is a proper walled towne, standing 8 myles est from Wighton, & not farr from the river of Hull, vppon a creek digged with mans hand from the said river.

Kingstowne vppon Hull (comonly called *Hull*) is a proper walled towne, well traded with shippes & marchandize, standing whereas the said river of Hull falleth into the Humber.

Headon standeth in the countrey called Holderness, 4 myles est from Hull, vppon a small river, which 2 myles thence falleth into the Humber

*Forrests

Pickering Forrest	Knaresborow Forrest	Langstrethdale Chase
Gautress Forrest	Lune Forrest	Hatfeld Chase
Swaledale Forrest	Bowland Forrest	Barden Chase
Aplegarth Forrest	The New Forrest	Bishoppsdale Chase

Castells

York, 2	Vpsall	Bowes
Richmond	Bolton	Conisburg
Midlham	Hornby	Sandall
Raunswath	Gilling	Wresill
Hatlesey	Slingsby	Wilton
Skelton	Crake	Wilton
Kilton	Hilderskill	Harwood
Moulgraue	Sherifhutton	Cawood
Wharlton	Skipton	Skarborow
Armanthwate	Pountfret	Hull
Sigston	Sheafeld	Tickhill

Abbais which sometime were

Mountgrace	Wickam	Geruis, in Richmondshyre
Fountains	Riuis	Rasdale
Handale	Marton	Watton
Growmond	Biland	

*DURHAM

[Coat of Arms of the Bishoprie of Durham at top see Plate II]

The Bishopprick of Durham was made a Countie Pallatyn by King Richard the First, who sold the same to the Bishopp, & created him Erle therof. It is 3 cornerd. On the est it hath the sea, from the Tyne to the Teese which is about 25 myles, on the south the said river of Teese devydeth it from Yorkshyre, all the course of it, which is about 40 myles, on the north it hath Northumberland, which syde is about 34 myles, the west corner toucheth vppon Yorkshyre, Westmerland, Cumberland, & Northumberland. In which countrey (besydes the cittie of Durham) there is 5 market townes, 72 parish churches, & 9 castells.

*[Coat of Arms of the town of Durham at top see Plate II]

Durham (as some hold opinion) should be called Deirham, because it was in tymes past the cheiffest towne of that kingdome, in Northumberland, which was called Deira. It is enuironed almost round about with the river of Were, which springeth in the west corner of the countrey, & passeth through the middest therof, directly est, vntill it come to Bishopps-Auckland, where it torneth north to Durham, Lumley, & Bedick, and then torneth agayne towards the est, & falleth into the sea, not farr from Weremouth.

Hartlepoole is a proper litle towne, standing in the sea, vppon a peninsula, which is a myle in compasse, and hath a prety port or hauen for shipps. It is about xj myles southest from Durham.

*Darlington (comonly called *Darrington*) is 13 myles south from Durham, in the way to London, vppon a small river named Skeen, which 2 myles thence falleth into the Teese.

Bishopps Auckland standeth vppon the Were, about 7 myles southwards from Durham.

Staynderp is 6 myles south southwest from Bishopps Auckland, vppon a small river, which 3 myles thence falleth into the Teese, and not farr from the towne standeth Raby Castell

Barnard-Castle standeth vppon *the* Teese, 5 myles southwest from Stayndorp

Forrests

Teesdale Forrest part of yt lyeth in Yorkshyre

Castells

Durham	Stocton	Brandspeth
Rauensworth	Raby	Hilton
Lumley	Barnard Castell	Witton

*WESTMERLAND

[Two Coats of Arms at top see Plate XIII, Nos 13 and 14]

Westmerland is but a litle countrey, and is enclosed on *the* est with Yorkshyre, & on *the* west with Cumberland, and hath Lancashyre on *the* south. The length from *the* north to the south is 30 myles, the breadth 16, in some places more & in some lesse. In which countrey there is 4 market townes, 8 castells, and 40 parish churches, besydes villages, & gentlemens howses

Appelby is *the* shyre towne of Westmerland, and standeth in *the* northend of the countrey, vppon *the* river of Eden, which ronneth from thence to Carlile

Kirkby-Staphen standeth vppon *the* said river, 7 myles southest from Appelby, & within 4 myles of Yorkshyre

Kirkby-Lansdale standeth vppon *the* river Lan (which ronneth from thence to Lancaster), 20 myles south southwest from Kirkby-Stephen, and within a myle of Lancashyre

Kirkby-Kendall (comonly called *Kendall*) standeth vppon *the* river of Ken, 8 myles northwest from Kirkby Landale

Forrests

Mallerstang Forrest, on *the* est syde of the countrey
Whinfeld Forrest, on *the* north, is a litle thing palled about

Castells

| Appleby | Hartley | Pendragon | Kendall |
| Howgill | Brougham | Bewley | Burgh |

*CUMBERLAND

[Three Coats of Arms at top see Plate XVI, Nos 5 to 7]

Cumberland is twise as bigg as Westmerland, and reacheth from the north to *the* south in length 55 myles. In the middest it is 30 myles brode, but toward ech end it is narrower. On the northwest it toucheth vppon Scotland, on the northest it hath Northumberland on *the* est Westmerland, on *the* southest it hath a peece of Lancashyre, namely Fournes Fells, and on *the* west it hath the Irish Sea. In which countrey (besydes *the* cittie of Carlile) there is viij market townes, 30 castells, 117 parish churches, with 9 chapells, which is in all 126, besydes gentlemens howses, & villages

*[Coats of Arms of Erls of Carlisle at top see Plate XV]

Carlile is an ancient cittie, standing vppon *the* river of Eden, which springeth in Mallerstang Forrest in Westmerland, & ronneth to Pendragon Castell, Kirkby Steuen, Musgraue, Appleby, Buley Castell, lastly meeteth with *the* Vlles, & there entreth through Cumberland to Kirkoswald, Armanthwate, Corby Castell, Linstock Castell, and at Carlile taketh in a river on ech syde, & at *the* west end of *the* cittie the third, named Cauda, from which place to Rowcliff Castell is 3 myles, where it meeteth with dyvers other waters & is 2 myles brode at a full sea, from which place to the meane sea is about 10 myles

*Brampton standeth in the countrey called Gilsland, 7 myles northest from Carlile

Penrith standeth vppon the river of Viles, which parteth Cumberland from Westmerland, about 14 myles southest from Carlile

Keswick standeth vppon Darwen Mere (out of which Mere the river Darwen springeth), wherin are 2 or 3 litle ilandes, wherof one belongeth to them that have the copper mynes hard by the towne, and is 18 myles southward from Carlile, & 14 southwest from Penreth

Ravenglass standeth hard by the sea, betwene the mouthes of two rivers which meete there, 16 myles south southwest from Keswik

Egremond standeth in Copeland, 10 myles northwest from Ravenglass, vppon a river, which 4 myles south from thence falleth into the sea, and yet the towne on the west syde hath the sea within 2 myles of yt

Wirkington is 8 myles north from Egremond, and standeth on the mouth of the river Darwen, which cometh from Keswik

Cokermouth standeth wherers the river Coker ffalleth into the Darwen, 5 myles est from Wirkinton, and lyke distance from the sea

*Ierby is 7 myles northest from Cokermouth, in the way to Carlile, 12 myles southwest from Carlile, vppon the head of a small river named Elne, which 10 myles from thence falleth into the sea

Forrests

Westward Forrest	Copeland Forrest	Inglewood Forrest

Castells

Carlile	Daker	Graistock
Bewcastell	Drumbrug	Blencrake
Askerton	Petterell Wray	Emleton
Scalby	Rose Castell	Lorton
Linstock	Wulsty	Harinton
Corby	Westward	Millum
Naworth	Haton	Irton
Castell Carrock	Highyate	Ousby
Roweliff	Kirkoswald	St Bees
Armanthwate	Thelcot	St Johns
Cannonby		

*NORTHUMBERLAND

[Four Coats of Arms at top see Plate V, Nos 8 to 11]

Northumberland was in tymes past a kingdome but then it contayned all the countrey from Humber to the Scottish Frith, and yet as it is, it is one of the greatest shyres in England On the northwest it is seperated from Scotland by the Cheviot Hills, & on the north by the river of Twede, on the est it hath the sea, on the south the bishopprick of Durham, and on the southwest Cumberland The length therof, from the north to the south, is 54 myles, the breadth at the south end, & in the middest, is 30 myles, but the more northward it goeth, the more narrower it is It hath 10 market townes 35 castells, & 100 parish churches, besydes chapells, gentlemens howses, and villages

*[Coat of Arms of the town of Newcastle at the top see Plate II]

Newcastell is a brave towne, walled about, standing vppon the river of Tyne (which there parteth Northumberland from the Bishopprick of Durham), distant about 6 myles from the sea It hath 4 parish churches, besydes Gatesyde, which is on the other syde of the water

Hexham (called in Latin, Hagulstadium), standeth on the south syde of the river of Tyne, 14 myles west from Newcastell, and was in tymes past a shyre towne of all that countrey yet called Hexhamshyre, which of late yeares by Act of Parliament was vnited to Northumberland

Haltwesell is 12 myles west from Hexham, within 4 myles of Cumberland, and standeth vppon the South Tyne, which a litle aboue Hexham meeteth with the North Tyne

Chipchase towne & castell standeth vppon the North Tyne, 6 myles northwest from Hexham

Morpeth is 12 myles north from Newcastell, & standeth vppon the river of Wanspeck, which 6 myles thence falleth into the sea

Warkworth standeth vppon the river of Coket, which a myle from thence falleth into the sea, and 3 myles from the mouth therof is Coket Iland

Alnwik standeth vppon the river of Ale, which 4 myles thence falleth into the sea, & is 5 myles northwest from Warkworth, in the way from Barwik to York

Chillingham is 7 myles northwest from Alnwik, and standeth vppon the river of Bromish, which some call in Latin, Bernicia, of which river the kingdome of Bernitia (as they affirme) should take name

Norham towne & castell standeth vppon the Twede, 5 myles southwest from Barwik

Barwik is a stronge towne standing on the north syde of the Twede, which not farr of falleth into the sea The territory of Barwik, which belongeth to England, on the further syde of the Twede, is 3 myles long, and two myles brode

[leaf 121]

[leaf 121v]

Castells

Newcastle	Thirlwall	Dunstaburg
Tynemouth	Simonsborne	Edlingham
Hexham	Chipchase	Chillingham
Pruddo	Haughton	Bambrow
Biwell	Swinborne	Horton
Belsey	Morpeth	Ford
Ogle	Bottell	Wark
Langley	Witton	Ftall
Willimotswik	Witherington	Norham
Aydon	Warkworth	Barwik
Bellister	Cortington	Dala
Blekensopp	Harbottell	

And thus, having made an end with all the Shyres in England, let vs proceed with those in Wales

[leaf 122]

*WALES

[Three Coats of Arms at top see Plate VIII, Nos 1 to 3]

All *Wales* (as it is now) is litle bigger then Yorkshyre It is, from St Donets, in Glamorganshyre, to the northmost part of Anglisea, about 120 myles, at the south end it is 100 myles brode, at the north end 60, and in the middest but 36 The countrey is full of hilles & mountains, & nothing so well inhabited as other partes of England, ffor I fynd to be in all Wales but 56 market townes, 659 parish churches, and about 76 chapells There is [in] all 13 shyres, wherof 7 are in South Wales, & 6 in North Wales

**Monmouthshire* hath Glocestershire on the est, the Seuern sea on the south, Glamorganshyre and Brecknockshyre on the west, & Herefordshyre on the north It is from the north to the south about 24 myles long, and the breadth 20, in some places more, & in some lesse In which countrey there is 6 market townes, 132 parish churches, & about 10 chapells The river of Wye parteth it from Glocestershyre, the river of Romney from Glamorganshyre, & the river of Monmow from Herefordshyre

[leaf 122v]

Monmouth ys the towne which geveth name to the whole shyre, and standeth where as the river of Monmow falleth into the Wye, distant 12 myles south southeast from Hereford, & 16 west southwest from Glocester

Abergueny is a proper towne, standing 10 myles west from Monmouth, & within 3 myles of Brecknockshyre, vppon the river of Vsk, which springeth at the Black Mountaine, in the very vttermost end of Brecknockshyre, & passeth through the middest of the same shyre estwards to Brecknock, Penketh, Langonider, Langattock, & after entreth into Monmouthshyre, passing by Abergueny, Vsk, Carlion, & Newport, where not farr of it falleth into the Severn sea

Vsk standeth in the middest of Monmouthshyre, vppon the said river of Vsk, 7 myles southest from Abergueny

Carlion standeth vppon the said river of Vsk, 6 myles south from the towne of Vsk

Newport standeth also vppon the said river of Vsk, 2 myles from Carlion, & within 3 myles of the Seuern sea

Chepstow (called in Latin, Strigulia) is a famous towne & castell, standing vppon the river of Wye, which 2 myles from thence falleth into the Seuern

Forrests

Wieswood Chase, by Monmouth

Castells

Monmouth	Newport	Matharn
Skenfrith	Grenfeld	Chepstow
Grismond	Bishton	Lanuair
Whitcastell	Penhow	Dinham
Ragland	Strogle	Caldicote
Carlion	Portskeriet	The Old Castle

*GLAMORGANSHIRE

Glamorganshire taketh name of one Morgan, who above 2000 yeares past was there slayne by his cosin Cunedag, King of Brittains, as the Walsh cronicles report It hath on the south the Seuern sea, on the west Carmardenshire, on the north Brecknockshyre, & on the est Monmouthshyre The length from the est to the west is 40 myles, the breadth at the est end is 20 myles, but the west end is much narower, ffor the last part therof, called Westgowre, is not above 5 myles brode In this countrey I fynd to be 7 market townes, 128 parish churches, with 6 chapells But it hath mo castells then any other shyre in England or in Wales The south syde of the countrey, along the Seuern sea, is well in-habited & replenished with townes & castells, but the north syde is full of mountains

Cardiff is the cheifest towne in Glamorganshyre, and standeth on the est banck of the river Taf, which 2 myles thence falleth into the Severn sea, & is within 2 myles of Monmouthshyre

Landaff standeth on the other syde of the same river, a myle above Cardiff, and is a cittie, because it hath a bishopp, who hath vnder hym Glamorganshyre, Monmouthshyre, Brecknockshyre, & Radnorshyre

Cowbridge is 8 myles west from Cardif, & standeth vppon a small river named Thaw, which 5 myles thence falleth into the Seuern sea

Bridgend is 5 myles westwards from Cowbridge, and standeth vppon the river of Ogmore, which 4 myles thence falleth into the Seuern sea

Aberauon standeth on the mouth of the river Auon, 7 myles westwards from Bridgend

Neath is 4 myles northwest from Aberauon, and standeth vppon the river of Neath, which litle more then 2 myles thence falleth into the Seuern sea

Swansey is 5 myles southwest from Neath, 6 directly west from Aberauon, and standeth vppon the mouth of the river Tawy, which there falleth into the Severn sea

Castells

Cardif	Lanquian	Kethligain
Landaff	Penllin	Kenfeag
St Fagans	Lanmais	Loghor
St George	Landogh	Webley
Menech	Landow	Landewy
Gwennow	St Donets	Penrise
Winston	Treer	Pennarth
Sily, or Sully	Caerfily	Oxwich
Barry	Morlash	Oistermouth
Funmon	Cothy	Castell Coch
Porkery	Ogmore	Denis Powis
Penmark	Newcastle	Tallauant
Neath		

BRECKNOCKSHYRE

Brecknockshire is 3 square, & every square is about 25 myles It hath Glamorganshyre on the south, Cardiganshyre on the west, Radnorshyre on the north, Herefordshire, & Monmouthshire on the est In it are 3 market townes, & 66 parish churches

Brecknoc (called in Walsh, Aberhodni) standeth whereas the river of Hodni falleth into the Vsk, & in the middest of the shyre

Bealt standeth vppon the Wye, which there parteth Brecknoeshire from Radnorshire, xj myles north from Brecknock

Hay standeth also vppon the Wye, 10 myles est from Bealt, & toucheth vppon Herefordshire

Castells

Brecknock	Blainllinuy	Tretoure
Dinas	Lanthew	Langoid
Broinclis	Trecastell	Penketh

CARMARDENSHYRE

Carmarthenshire hath Brecknockshyre on the est, Glamorganshyre on the southest, the Seuern Sea on the south, Penbrokshyre on the west, and Cardiganshyre on the northwest The length therof is from the southwest to the northest 30 myles, the breadth 20, in some places more, & in some lesse In which countrey there is 6 markett townes, & 85 parish churches

Carmarthen is a proper walled towne, standing vppon the river of Towy, which 6 myles south from thence falleth into the Seuern sea

Landillauaure standeth vppon the said river of Towy, 10 myles northest from Carmarden

Langadock standeth also vppon the said river of Towy, 3 myles northest from Landillauaure

Lan-ymthefiy standeth also vppon the said river of Towy, 5 myles north from Langadock

Kidwely standeth at the confluence of 2 rivers, within a myle of the sea, and is distant 6 myles south southest from Carmarden

Lauellhy standeth vppon a litle creek within a myle of the sea, 5 myles est southest from Kidwily, and within 2 myles of Glamorganshyre

Forrests
Cardith Forrest

Castells

| Carmarthen | Lacharn | Kidwily | Careg |
| Deneuer | Lanstephen | Druslone | Memlin |

[leaf 127b contains Coats of Arms of Earls of Pembroke see Plate IV]

*PENBROKSHYRE

Penbrokshire is the vttermost part of all Wales towards the west, and is compassed round about with the sea, saving on the northest it toucheth vppon Cardiganshyre, & Carmardenshyre The length therof from the north to the south is about 26 myles, the breadth 10, 12, 16, and in brodest place not above 18 myles In which countrey there is 5 market townes, and 148 parish churches

Penbroke standeth vppon one of the gulfes of Milford Hauen, about 6 myles from the mouth of the said hauen But on the southest syde it hath the sea within 2 myles, and is enclosed with 2 litle brookes which meet on the west syde of the towne & there make the said gulf, which is about halff a myle brode, & so contineweth for the space of 2 myles, & then falleth into Milford Hauen, much narrower, and is there called Penner mouth

Tenby (comonly called *Fishing Tenby*), standeth vppon the sea, compassed almost round about therwith 6 myles est from Penbrok, & 2 myles south from it lyeth Calday Iland

Harford (comonly called *Harford West*) is 7 myles northwest from Penbroke, and standeth vppon the river of Duggleddy, which 4 myles thence meeteth with the Clothy, & so fall into Milford Hauen

St Dauids standeth on the very vttermost point of all Wales, within a myle of the sea, & was in tymes past an archbishoppnck, & is yet a bishoppnck, vnder whose dioces is Penbrokshyre, & Carmardenshyre Three myles from St Dauids lyeth Ramsey Iland, & 6 myles south from thence lyeth dyvers other ilands, but the cheifest are Scalme, Stockholme, Gresholme, Gatesholme, &c

Fiskard standeth on the mouth of a small river named Gwyne, 10 myles northest from St Dauids

Neaport is 5 myles northest from Fiskard, and standeth vppon the river of Neuern, 2 myles from the sea

Forrests

| Codrath Forrest | Nabarth Forrest | Kilgarron Forrest |

Castells

Penbroke	Nabarth	Picton
Carew	Kilgarron	Lanhaddon
Marberbury	Roch	Benton
Redcastell	Wiston	Walwin
Haus	Newcastell	Haroldston

There are dyvers others that beare the names of castells, but whether they have castells or no I know not, as Castle Male, Castlebigh Castle Henry, Castle Marton

*CARDIGANSHYRE

Cardiganshire is in proportion lyke a halff moone It is in length from the north to the south 30 myles, the breadth in the middest is 15 myles, & at ech end but 6 It hath the Irish Sea on the west, Mermothshyre on the north, Montgomoryshyre on the northest, Radnor & Brecknocshyres on the est, Carmardenshyre on the southest, and Penbrokshyre on the south In which countrey there is 4 market townes, and about 67 parish churches

Cardigan standeth on the south end of the shyre within 3 myles of the sea, vppon the river of Tivy, which there parteth Cardiganshyre from Penbrokeshyre

DESCRIPTION OF ENGLAND   57

Lanbeder standeth vppon *the* said river of Tuy, *which* there parteth Cardiganshyre from Carmardenshyre, 18 myles northest from Cardigan

Tregaron standeth vppon *the* said river, 7 myles north from Lanbeder

Aberystwith is xj myles northwest from Tregaron, & standeth vppon *the* river of Ridall, which springeth at Plinlimon Hill (at *which* hill *the* Seuern & *the* Wye also do spring), and beneath *the* towne the Ridall meeteth with the Istwith, & therby falleth into *the* sea

Forrests

Rescob Forrest   Lanbeder Forrest

*RADNORSHYRE   *[leaf 130b]

Radnorshire is *the* least shyre in South Wales. It is 3 square, & euery square is about 20 myles. It hath Montgomoryshyre on *the* north, Shropshire on *the* northest, Herefordshyre on *the* est, Brecknockshyre on *the* south, and the west end toucheth on Cardiganshyre. In it are 4 market townes, & about 50 parish churches

Radnor (comonly called *New Radnor*, for diffrence of Old Radnor, 2 myles from thence) standeth in *the* est end of the shyre, vppon *the* head of a small river named Somergill, *which* ronneth from thence to Old Radnor, and so entring into Herefordshyre, falleth into *the* Lug beneath Prestain

Prestaine is 4 myles northest from Radnor, and standeth vppon the river of Lug, so nigh to Herefordshire that I thinck some part of *the* towne standeth therein

Knighton is 4 myles north northwest from Prestaine, and standeth vppon the river Teme, which there parteth Radnorshyre from Shropshyre

Rayadergowy (that is to say *the* fall of the Wye) standeth vppon the Wye, 12 myles west from Radnor

*Forrests   *[leaf 131]

Radnor Forrest   The Forrest of Knuckells.   The Forrest of Bletuach

Castells

Radnor	Ceuenlles	Boughrud	Colwin
Dinbod	Payn	Norton	Aber-edway

Having finished the 7 shyres in South Wales, now have at the 6 in North Wales

*MONTGOMORYSHYRE   *[leaf 131b]

Montgomoryshire is in a maner round, or rather egg forme having 30 myles in length & 20 in breadth. It hath on *the* est Shropshyre, on *the* southest Radnorshyre, on *the* southwest Cardiganshyre, on the northwest Mermothshyre, and on *the* north a litle peec of Denbighshyre. In it are 6 market townes & about 50 parish churches

Montgomery standeth on *the* est part of *the* shyre, within a myle of Shopshyre, & lyke distance from *the* Seuern

Poole (comonly called *Walsh Poole*) is 5 myles north from Montgomory, and standeth vppon a small broke named Lleding, *which* hard by falleth into *the* Seuern

Lanuilling is 8 myles northwest from Poole, within 3 myles of Denbighshyre, & within 4 myles of Shropshyre

Newtown standeth vppon *the* Seuerne, 6 myles southwest from Montgomory

Llan Idlos standeth also vppon *the* Seuern, 8 myles southwest from Newtowne, *[leaf 132] & lyke distance from *the* very head of *the* Seuern

Machenllet standeth on *the* very west end of *the* shyre, 16 myles northwest from Lan Idlos, vppon *the* river of Deuy, *which* there parteth Montgomoryshyre from Mermothshire, and within 8 myles of *the* meane Irish Sea

Castells

Montgomory	Gogh	Machauern
Engerrimon	Doleuoren	Caersuse

S

*MERINOTHSHYRE

Merinothshire is 3 square, and every square is about 25 myles. On the west square it hath the Irish Sea, on the northwest & north Carnaruanshyre & Denbighshyre, on the southest a part of Denbighshyre, so much of it as lyeth south of the river of Dee, and on the south corner Montgomoryshyre, & Cardiganshyre, ffrom which last it is seperated by the river Deuy, which parteth North Wales from South Wales. In it are 3 market townes, & 38 parish churches

Harlech (which is the cheiffest towne in the shyre) standeth at the west end of the countrey, vppon the sea syde. But Towen Merioneth (wherof the countrey taketh name) is a village standing in the south corner of the shyre

Dolgell is 10 myles southest from Harlech, and standeth vppon a river named Auon, which a myle beneath the towne meeteth with another as bigg as it selffe, & 6 myles thence fall into the sea, at Barmouth

Bala standeth vppon the river of Dee, nere vnto the Lake Tegill (out of which the said river cometh), about 14 myles northest from Dolgelh

Castells

| Barmouth | Kemmer | Thchery |

*CARNARUANSHYRE

Carnaruanshire is the vttermost part westward of North Wales, and lyke a promontory into the sea, reaching from the river of Conway to the Isle of Bardsey on the west end, which is about 34 myles. At the est end it is 18 myles brode, but the further it stretcheth into the sea the narrower it is. On the north lyeth the Isle of Anglisea, on the est it is seperated by the river of Conway from Denbighshyre, and on the south it toucheth on Merinothshyre. In which countrey there is 5 market townes, & about 60 parish churches

Carnaruan is a strong towne & castell, founded by K. Edward the first, who subdewed North Wales, and standeth on the north syde of the countrey, vppon the mouth of the river Saint, which there falleth into the Menay, over against Anglisea

Bangor is a bishopps seat, and standeth vppon the said Menai, 7 myles northest from Carnaruan, and 3 from Bewmaris in Anglisea. The Bishopp of Bangor hath vnder his diocess Carnaruanshyre, Anglisea, & Merinothshyre

Conway (called in Walsh, Aber-Conwy) standeth on the mouth of the river Conwy, about 8 myles estwards from Bangor. Here at Conway, Carnaruanshyre goeth over the river, and obtayneth a great parcell of ground called Ormshead Point, wherein are 4 parish churches, besydes gentlemens howses, & villages

Newin standeth on the north syde of the shyre vppon the sea syde, 13 myles southwest from Carnaruan

Pullely standeth on the south syde of the countrey, vppon a creeke nere the sea syde, 5 myles estwards from Newin. Betwene these two townes ys the narrowest place of Carnaruanshyre

Castells

Carnaruan	Caer Iernrode	Dinas Orueg
Conway	Sinado	Dinas Dinlley,
Dolathelan	Delbadern	Criketh

*ANGLISEA

Anglisea is an iland, cut from Wales, with a small arme of the sea called Menai, which in some places is but halff a myle brode. The island it selffe is in a maner round, ffrom the est to the west is 20 myles, and from the north to the south is about 16 myles. In it are 2 market townes, & 68 parish churches

Beumaris is a proper towne & castell, standing on the est end of the countrey, 3 myles north from Bangor, & 8 west from Conway

Newburgh standeth on the south corner of the iland, within 2 myles of the sea, & as farr from the Menai, litle more then 3 myles from Carnaruan

Aberfraw was in old tyme the cheiffest Towne of all Wales, but now I thinck it be no market towne. It standeth within a myle of the sea, 4 myles northwest from Newburgh

Castells

Bewmaris

*DENBIGHSHYRE *[leaf 135b]

Denbighshire stretcheth in length from Conway vntill it come within 2 myles of Oswestry, which is from the northwest to the southest about 32 myles, at ech end it is 16 myles brode, but in the middest in some places not passing 5. On the west it hath Carnaruanshyre, on the north the Irish Sea, on the northest Flintshyre, on the est Cheshyre & a parcell of Flintshyre on the southest Shropshyre & Montgomoryshyre, and on the south Merinothshyre. It hath 3 market townes, & about 55 parish churches

Denbigh is a proper towne, walled about, standing in a pleasant valley, on the *[leaf 136] northsyde of the countrey, 12 myles southwest from Flint, & within 3 myles of Flintshyre

Ruthin towne & castell (whereof the Lord Gray of Ruthin taketh name) standeth in the middest of the shyre, vppon the river Cluyd, 6 myles southest from Denbighshyre

Wrixham standeth on the est corner of the shyre, within 3 myles of Cheshyre, vppon a litle brooke which ronneth into the Dee, and is 10 myles from Ruthin

Castells

| Denbigh | Holt | Chirck |
| Ruthin | Dinas-Bran | |

*FLINTSHYRE *[leaf 136b]

Flintshire lyeth along the mouth of the river of Dee (which seperateth it from Cheshyre) and hath Denbighshire on the southwest, so that the length therof from the northwest to the southest is 20 myles, the breadth at ech end is 6 myles, but in the middest it is not above 3 myles brode. In which countrey I fynd to be 2 market townes & 20 parish churches. But there is one parcell more of Flintshyre (lying on the southsyde of the river Dee) which is compassed on the est & south with Shropshyre, having Cheshyre on the north, & Denbighshyre on the west, which is 7 myles long & 6 brode, wherein is 4 parish churches & 2 chapells, which maketh in all 24 parish churches

Flint towne & castell standeth on the west banke of the river of Dee (which *[leaf 137] river is there 3 myles brode), and is 10 myles distant west northwest from Chester

Sainct Assaph is 9 myles west from Flint, 5 north from Denbigh. It is called in Walsh, Lan Elwy, and standeth betwene 2 rivers, Clyd & Elwy, so nere to Denbighshyre that I thinck some part of the towne standeth therein. The Bishopp of St Assaph hath vnder hym part of Denbighshyre, part of Flintshyre, & the Ile of Prestholme. The rest of the said shyres are in the Diocess of the Bishopp of Chester

Castells

| Flint | Treer | Harden, alias Hawarden |
| Rudlan | Yowley | |

[leaf 137b is blank]

*ISLANDS *[leaf 138]

Now that we have ronne over all England & Wales, let vs speake a word or two of such Ilandes as be inhabited, & belonging to the Crowne of England, and of such townes & parish churches as be therein

WIGHT

The *Isle of Wight* is called in Latin, Vectis, and belongeth to Hamshyre for temporall jurisdiction, and in spirituall causes yeldeth obaydience to the seat of Winchester, whereof it is a deanry. It is in some places 6 myles distant from the mayne land, and in some places not passing a myle. In forme it representeth almost an egg, being in length 20 myles, & in breadth 10, wherein is one market towne, called Newport, standing in the middest therof, vppon a small river, which is made so brode & depe that at a full sea both botes & shipps may come from the sea on the northsyde to the towne, which is 5 myles, with which towne it hath 36 other townes, villages, & castells, besydes 27 parish churches. Amongst which castells, Caerbro, standing on a hill, almost in the middest of the island, ys the most greatest, ancientest, & most famous.

[leaf 138] *These Islands do ly vppon the coast of France, and the inhabitants therof do speake French, but are vnder the crowne of England, whose names do follow

Gersey	St Hilaries	Burho
Garnsey	The Cornet	Brehoe
Alderney	The Herme	Githo
Serk		

Gersey is the greatest of all these, having 30 myles in compasse, and is 21 myles distant from Garnsey. It hath 12 parish churches, with a college, which hath a deane & prebendes.

Garnsey had in tymes past 5 religious howses, & 9 castells, but now there is but one parish church standing in the same.

Alderney is 7 myles about, and hath a prety towne therin with a parish church, and hath great plenty of corne, cattell, conies & wild foule, wood only lacketh.

[leaf 139] *Serk is 6 myles about, and hath another adnexed to it by an isthumus, wherein was a religious howse, and great store of conies.

Sainct Hillarius is fast vppon Gersey, wherein some tymes was a monastary.

The Cornet hath a castell, and is not passing an arrow shoot from Gersey.

The Herme is 4 myles about, wherein in tymes past was a chanonry, which after was converted to a howse of Franciscans.

Burho is otherwise called *The Isle of Ratts*, because of the huge plenty of ratts which are found there, althowgh otherwise it be replenished with great store of conies, betwene whom and the ratts (as some thinck) those which we call Turky conies are produced.

[leaf 139 v] *THE ISLES OF SORLINGUES

The Isles of Sorlingues (comonly called *The Silles*) do ly in the sea, 20 myles westward from the point of Cornwall, and are in number 147, wherof ech one is greater or lesser then another. But there are 20 of them, which for their greatnes & comodities exceed all the rest. Therto (if you respect their position) they are scituate in maner of a circle or ring, having a huge lake or portion of the sea in the middest of them.

The first & greatest of all is *St Maries Ish*, which is about 5 myles over, or 9 myles in compasse; therein is a parish church, with a poore towne belonging therto of 60 howscholdes, besydes a castell. It hath plenty of corne, conies, wild foule, wild swans, puffins, gulles, cranes, & other kyndes of foule, in great abundance.

The Agnus Isle is 6 myles over, and hath one towne or parish within the same, of 5 or 6 howsholdes, besydes no small store of hoggs, & conies of sundry coulers.

The Annett hath great store of hoggs & conies.

[leaf 140] *The *Rusco* is very nere so great as St Maries Isle, & hath within it a fort, & a parish church, great store of conies & wild foule.

The Brier hath a village, castell, & parish church.

DESCRIPTION OF ENGLAND

St Lides hath a parish church, dedicated to *that* Sainct

The Tian is a great island, furnished with a parish church, & great store of conies

Mintersand
Smithsound
Suartigan } These are replenished with conies & wild garlik, but void of wood & other comodities, saving a short kind of grasse, & here & there some firzes, whereon those conies do feed
Rousnian
Rousnias
Cregrem

Rat Island hath such store of monstrous ratts, that if horses or other beasts do chaunce to come or be left there, are sure to be devoured

Moncarthat	*Arning*	*Vollis,* 1
Inis Welseck	*St Martins.*	*Sunzerke*
Suethiall	*Knolicon th.*	*Vollis,* 2
Anwall	*Smullmer*	*Arthurs Isle*
Notho	*Guinillmer*	*Neuech*
The Round Island	*Men Witham*	*Gothiors*

These yeld a short kind of grass for conies, and in *the* great are sundry lakes, with great store of wild foule

Lundy lyeth in the Seuern Sea, 16 myles from Wales & 12 from Deuonshyre, whereof it is a parcell It is 6 myles long, & in[1] some 2 or 3 myles brode, & hath a towne with a parish of 40 howsholds

Calday hath a parish church with a spyre steple, & belongeth to Penbrokshyre

Ramsey is 5 myles long & 3 brode
Scalme, magna,
Scalme, parua, } These, with dyvers other lesser, do belong to *the* county of Penbrok, and in spirituall matters to *the* Bishopp of St Dauids
Stockholme,
Gresholme,

Bardsey belongeth to Carnaruanshyre, is 6 myles long & 4 brode

Islernd,
Inislig, } belong to Anglisea, & ly hard by it

Prestholme lyeth also by Anglisea, is 3 myles long & 1 brode

Helbree belongeth to Cheshyre, is but a myle over

Wauency, & divers other less, ly vppon *the* coast of Lancashyre

Lindisfarne (now called *Holy Iland*) lyeth not farr from Barwik, and was in tymes past a bishopps seat, from whence it was removed to Durham

Farne, & dyvers others lying about it, do belong to Northumberland

Coket lyeth also by Northumberland, over against *the* mouth of *the* river Coket

[Coat of Arms of the Isle of Man at top see Plate II]

The Isle of Man lyeth in the sea, in a maner halff way betwene England & Ireland, and was in tymes past a kingdome At this present it belongeth to *the* Erle of Darby It hath a bishopp, subiect vnder *the* Archbishopp of York It is greater then Anglisea by a third part, wherein in tymes past were 1300 famalies, of which 960 were in *the* west halff, & *the* rest in *the* other But now (through joyning howse to howse & land to land) *the* halff therof is diminished There are 2 rivers in *the* same, whose heads do joyne so nere that they seeme to part the island in two The cheiffest townes therein are these

Rushen	St Michaell	Pala Salla
Dunglass	St Andrew	Kirk St Mary
Holme	Kirk Christ	Kirk Concane
St Brydes	Kirk Louell	Kirk Malu
Bala Cury, *the* Bishopps Howse	St Michaes Kirk Santon	Home

But of all these Rushen, with *the* Castell, is *the* strongest

[1] Thus in the MS

*It is also in recompence of wood (*which* there wanteth) endwed with dyvers prety rivers & fresh waters. It hath also dyvers hilles of name; also sundry fayre hauens, as Ramsey Hauen by north, Laxham Hauen by est, Port Iris by southwest, Port Home & Port Michaell by west. In lyke sort, there are dyvers litle Isletts, as the Calf of Man, on *the* south; the Pyle on the west, and St Michaells Isle in the gulf called Ratnothsway in *the* est. The shepe in this countrey are exceeding huge, well wolled, and their tayles of such greatnes as is almost incredible. In lyke sort are their hoggs in a maner monstrous. They have furthermore great store of barnacles breeding vppon their coasts (but yet not so great store as in Ireland), and do breed vppon old putrified pitched wood, as old shipps, ores, masts, & such lyke. But neither they nor the Irishmen can tell whether they be flesh or fish, ffor although their religious men vsed to eate them as fish, yet elswhere some have have byn troubled for eating them, as Heretiks & Lollards.

*There are divers countreis, islands, & other famous places in England (besydes these spoken of beffore), which shall follow in maner of *the* alphabeth, wherby you shall perceaue in what shyre euery one lyeth.

Austr, in Yorkshire	*Kistauen*, in Lincolnshyre
Axholme Island, in Lincolnshyre	*Lindsey*, in Lincolnshyre
Aundrues, in Lancashyre	*Louingland*, in Suffolk
Aueland Isle, in Somersetshyre	*Marshland*, in Norfolk
Blakay-more, in Yorkshyre	*Marshland*, in Yorkshyre
Cleueland, in Yorkshyre	*Meuege*, in Cornwall
Copeland, in Cumberland	*Muchney Ish*, in Somersetshyre
Canue Ilands, in Essex	*Netherdale*, in Yorkshyre
Canford Launds, in Dorcetshyre	*Oaney Ish*, in Kent
Cotswold, in Glocestershyre	*Purbeck Isle*, in Dorcetshyre
Dartmore, in Deuonshyre	*Portland Isle*, in Dorcetshyre
Dich-marsh, in Yorkshyre	*Richmondshyre*, in Yorkshyre
Ely Ish, in Cambridgeshyre	*Rosland*, in Cornwall
Einshohne-Vale, in Worcestershire, but part of yt lyeth in Glocestershyre	*Redsdale*, in Northumberland
	Rumney-Marsh, in Kent
	Salisbury-Playn, in Wiltshyre
Fournes Fells, in Lancashyre	*Shepey Ish*, in Kent
Gillsland, in Cumberland	*Tanet Ish*, in Kent
Gower, in Glamorganshyre	*Tindale*, in Northumberland
Graue Ish, in Kent	*Tunbridge Territory*, in Kent
Hallamshyre, in Yorkshyre	*Wirall*, in Cheshyre
Hexhamshyre, in Northumberland	*Winsdale*, in Yorkshyre
Holland, in Lincolnshyre	*Yorks-Wold*, in Yorkshyre
Holdernes, in Yorkshyre	

---

*BURGESES OF *THE* PARLIAMENT

THE NAMES OF COUNTIES, CITIES, BOROUGHS, AND PORTS, SENDING KNIGHTS, CITIZENS, BURGESES, & BARONS, TO *THE* PARLIAMENT OF ENGLAND

Bedfordshyre, knights	2	*Cambridshyre*, knights	2
The borow of Bedford	2	The borow of Cambridge	2
Buckinghamshyre, knights	2	*Cheshyre*, knights	2
The borow of Buckingham	2	The cittie of Chester	2
The borow of Wickam	2	*Cornwall*, knights	2
The borow of Alesbury	2	The boro of Launston	2
Barkshyre, knights	2	The borow of Leskerd	2
The borow of Windsor	2	The borow of Lestethiell	2
The borow of Reding	2	The borow of Dunheuet	2
The borow of Wallingford	2	The borow of Truro	2
The borow of Abbington	2	The borow of Bodman	2

The borow of Saltash	2	The borow of Boston	2
The borow of Helston	2	The borow of Grimsby	2
The borow of Camelford	2	The borow of Stamford	2
The borow of Port Low	2	The borow of Grantham	2
The borow of Grampound	2	*Lancashyre*, knights	2
The borow of Est Low	2	The borow of Lancaster	2
The borow of Piury	2	The borow of Preston	2
The borow of Tregunian	2	The borow of Lupoole	2
The borow of Trebenna	2	The borow of Newton	2
The borow of St Ices	2	The borow of Wigan	2
The borow of Foy	2	The borow of Clithero	2
The borow of German	2	*Leicestershyre*, knights	2
The borow of Michaell	2	The borow of Lecester	2
The borow of St Maries	2	*Middlesex*, knights	2
Cumberland, knights	2	The cittie of London	4
The cittie of Carlile	2	The cittie of Westminster	2
Darbyshyre, knights	2	*Northamptonshyre*, knights	2
The borow of Darby	2	The cittie of Peterborow	2
Denonshyre, knights	2	The borow of Northampton	2
The cittie of Excester	2	The borow of Brakley	2
The borow of Totnes	2	The borow of Higham Ferries	2
The borow of Plimouth	2	*Nottinghamshyre*, knights	2
The borow of Plimton	2	The borow of Nottingham	2
The borow of Barstable	2	The borow of Est Retford	2
The borow of Tauestoke	2	**Norfolk*, knights	2 *[leaf 144]
The borow of Dartmouth-Clifton & Hardnes	2	The cittie of Norwich	2
*Dorcetshyre, knights		The borow of Linn	2
The borow of Dorchester	2	The borow of Great Yermouth	2
The borow of Poole	2	The borow of Thetford	2
The borow of Lyme	2	The borow of Castell Rysing	2
The borow of Melcomb	2	*Northumberland*, knights	2
The borow of Waymouth	2	The borow of Newcastell	2
The borow of Burport	2	The borow of Morpeth	2
The borow of Shaftesbury	2	The borow of Barwik	2
The borow of Warham	2	*Oxfordshyre*, knights	2
Essex, knights		The cittie of Oxford	2
The borow of Colchester	2	The borow of Banbury	2
The borow of Maldon	2	The borow of Woodstock	2
Gloecestershyre, knights		*Rutland*, knights	2
The cittie of Glocester	2	*Surrey*, knights	
The borow of Ciceter	2	The borow of Southwark	2
Huntingtonshyre, knights	2	The borow of Gillford	2
The borow of Huntington	2	The borow of Blechinghgh	2
Hartfordshyre, knights		The borow of Rigate	2
The borow of St Albons	2	The borow of Gatton	2
Herefordshyre, knights		*Shropshyre*, knights	
The cittie of Hereford	2	The borow of Shrewsbury	2
The borow of Lemster	2	The borow of Bridgenorth	2
Kent, knights		The borow of Ludlow	2
The cittie of Canterbury	2	The borow of Wenlock	2
The cittie of Rochester	2	*Southamptonshyre*, knights	2
The borow of Maidston	2	The cittie of Winchester	2
The borow of Quinborow	2	The borow of Southampton	2
Lincolnshyre, knights	2	The borow of Portsmouth	2
The cittie of Lincolne	2	The borow of Petersfeld	2
		The borow of Stockbridge	2

The borow of Christs-Church	2
Somersetshyre knights	2
The cittie of Bristow	2
The cittie of Bath	2
The cittie of Wells	2
The borow of Taunton	2
The borow of Bridgewater	2
The borow of Minhead	2
Staffordshyre knights	2
The cittie of Lichfeld	2
The borow of Stafford	2
The borow of Newcastell	2
The borow of Tamworth	2
Suffolk, knights	2
The borow of Ipswich	2
The borow of Dunwich	2
The borow of Orford	2
The borow of Aldborowgh	2
The borow of Sudbury	2
The borow of Aye	2
Sussex knights [*leaf 145*]	2
The cittie of Chichester	2
The borow of Midhurst	2
The borow of Lewes	2
The borow of Shoram	2
The borow of Bramber	2
The borow of Stening	2
The borow of Grensted	2
The borow of Horsham	2
The borow of Arundell	2
Warwikshire knights	2
The cittie of Conentrie	2
The borow of Warwik	2
Westmerland, knights	2
The borow of Apelby	2
Wiltshire knights	2
The cittie of New-Salesbury	2
The borow of Wilton	2
The borow of Duneton	2
The borow of Hindon	2
The borow of Hetsbury	2
The borow of Westbury	2
The borow of Calne	2
The borow of Deuises	2
The borow of Chippenham	2
The borow of Malmsbury	2
The borow of Marlborow	2
The borow of Criklade	2
The borow of Great Bedwin	2
The borow of Lurgishall	2
The borow of Old Salesbury	2
The borow of Wotton Basset	2
Worcestershire knights	2
The cittie of Worcester	2
The borow of Durtwich	2
Yorkshire, knights	2
The cittie of York	2
The bo of Kingstown super Hull	2
The borow of Knaresborow	2
The borow of Scarborow	2
The borow of Rippon	2
The borow of Howdon	2
The borow of Borowbrigg	2
The borow of Thursk	2
The borow of Aldborow	2
The borow of Beuerley	2

WALES

Monmouthshyre, knights	2
The borow of Monmouth	1
Glamorganshyre, knights	1
The borow of Cardiff	1
Brecknockshire, knights	1
The borow of Brecknock	1
Carmardinshire, knights	1
The borow of Carmarden	1
Penbrokshyre, knights	1
The borow of Penbroke	1
Radnorshyre, knights	1
The borow of Radnor	1
Cardiganshyre, knights	1
The borow of Cardigan	1
Montgomeryshyre, knights [*leaf 145b*]	1
The borow of Montgomory	1
Merinothshyre, knights	1
The borow of Harlech	1
Carnaruanshyre, knights	1
The borow of Carnaruan	1
Anglesea, knights	1
The borow of Bewmaris	1
Denbighshyre, knights	1
The borow of Denbigh	1
Flintshyre, knights	1
The borow of Flint	1

BARONS OF THE PORTES

Hastings	2
Winchelsey	2
Ry	2
Rumney	2
Douer	2
Hyde	2
Sandwich	2

SOMMA TOTALIS OF THE COMON HOWSE

Knights	90
Cittezens	46
Burgeses	289
Barons	14
	439

*FAYRES

THE MONTH, DAY, & PLACE, OF ALL THE PRINCIPALL FAYRES KEPT IN ENGLAND

January

6   at Salesbary

25 { at Bristow
     at Grauesend, in Kent
     at Churchingford
     at Northalerton, where a fayre is kept euery Wensday from Christmas till June

February

1   at Bromley, in Kent
     at Linn, in Norfolk
     at Bath, in Somersetshire
     at Maidston, in Kent
     at Bickelsworth
     at Budworth, in Cheshyre
14   at Fauersham, in Kent
On Ashwensday
     at Lichfeld, in Staffordshire
     at Roiston, in Hartfordshire
     at Excester, in Deuonshire
     at Abbington, in Barkshire
     at Creeter, in Glocestershire
24   at Henley vppon Thamise, in Oxfordshire
     at Tewksbury, in Glocestershire

March

12 { at Stamford, in Lincolnshire
     at Sudbury, in Suffolk

13 { at Wye, in Kent
     at St Michalls Mount
     at Bodman, in Cornwall

The first Sonday in Lent
     at Grantham, in Lincolnshire
     at Salesbury, in Wiltshire
On Monday, beffore our Lady Day
     at Wisbich, in Cambridgeshire
     at Kendall, in Westmerland
     at Denbigh, in Wales
20 being St Cuthberts Day
     at Durham

25 { at Northampton
     at Maldon, in Essex
     at Great Chart, in Kent
     at New Castell
     at Huntington, euery Lady Day

*Aprill

5   at Wallingford, in Barkshire
7   at Darby
9   at Bickelsworth
     at Billingworth, the next Monday after
     at Euesholm, in Worcestershire
Tewsday in Easter week
     at Northflete, in Kent
     at Rochford, in Essex
     at Hitchin, in Hartfordshire
23   at Tamworth
     at Anthill, in Bedfordshire
     at Heningham, in Norfolk
     at Gilford, in Surrey
     at St Pombs, in Cornwall
22   at Stopford, in Cheshire
23   at Charing, } in Kent
     at Wrotham, }
     at Ipswich, in Suffolk
     at Darby
     at Dunmow, in Essex
26   at Tenterden, in Kent
The third Sonday after Easter
     a[t] Louth, in Lincolnshyre

May

1   at Rippon, in Yorkshire
     at Pern, in Cornwall
     at Oswestrie, in Shropshire
     at Lexfeld, in Suffolk
     at Stow on the Wold, in Glocestershire
     at Reading, in Barkshire
     at Leecester
     at Chelmsford, in Essex
     at Maidston, in Kent
     at Brickhill, in Buckinghamshire
     at Blakborn, in Lancashire
     at Congleton, in Cheshire
3   at Bramyard, in Herefordshire
     at Heningham, in Norffolk
     at Listow
7   at Beuerley, in Yorkshire
     at Newton, in Lancashire
     at Oxford
On Assension Day
     at Newcastell
     at Yerne
     at Bermicham, in Warwickshire
     at St Edes, in Huntingdonshire
     at Bishoppstratford, in Hartfordshire
     at Wicham, in Lancashire
     at Midlewich, } in Cheshire
     at Stopford, }

at Chapellfirth, in Darby*shire*
*On Whitson Even [f 147]
at Skipton vppon Craven
On Whitsonday
   at Rychill, or Richill
   at Gribby, & eue*ry* Wensday fortnight
   at Kingston vppon Thamise
   at Rachdale, in Lanca*shire*
   at Kirkby Stephen, in Westmer-
    land
On Monday in Whitson weke
   at Excester, in Denon*shire*
   at Darington, in Yorkshyre
   at Bradford, in Yorkshire
   at Rigate, in Surrey
   at Burton in Lansdale
   at Salford in Lancashire
   at Whitchurch, in Shrops*hire*
   at Cokermouth, in Cumb*erland*
   at Apelby in Westm*erland*
   at Bickelsworth
On Tewsday in Whitson week
   at Lewes, in Sussex
   at Rochford, in Essex
   at Canterbury, in Kent
   at Ormskirk, in Lanca*shire*
   at High Knutsford in Ches*hire*
   at Herith, in Westm*erland*
On Wensday in Easter week [*so in MS*]
   at Sandbar
On Trinyty Sonday
   at Kendall, in Westm*erland*
   at Rowell
On Corpus Christi Day
   at Prescot, in Lanca*shire*
   at Stopford, in Ches*hire*
   at St Annes
   at Newbery, in Barks*hire*
   at Couentry
   at St Edes, in Hunt*ingdonshire*
   at Bishopstratford, in Hartford-
    shire
   at Ross in Hereford*shire*
19 at Donstable in Bedford*shire*
   at Rochester, in Kent
29 at Cranbrok, in Kent
27 at Lenham in Kent
Thursday in Rogation week
   at Brasted, in Kent

June [f 147]
9 at Maidston, in Kent
11 at Okingham, in Barks*hire*
   at Newborow, in Lanca*shire*
   at Maxfeld, in Ches*hire*
   at Holt, in Denbighshire
23 On Midsomer Even
   at Shrewsbury
   at St Albones
24 On Midsomer Day
   at Heresham, in Kent,
   at Bedall
   at Strackstock
   at St Annes
   at Wakefeld
   at Colchester
   at Reding
   at Bedford
   at Barnwell, besyde Cambridge
   at Wollerhampton
   at Cranbrok
   at Glocester
   at Lincolne
   at Peterborow
   at Windsor
   at Harston, in Suff*olk*
   at Chester
   at Lancaster
   at Halifax
   at Ashborn, in Darbyshyre
27 at Folkston, in Kent
28 at Heteonne, in Kent
   at St Pombs, in Cornwall
29 On St Peters Day
   at Woodhurst
   at Marlborow in Wilts*hire*
   at Halesworth, in Suff*olk*
   at Wollerhampton, in Stafford*shire*
   at Petersfeld, in Hamshire
   at Lemster, in Hereford*shire*
   at Sudbury, in Suff*olk*
   at Gargrange
   at Bromley, in Lanca*shire*
   at Low Knutsford, in Ches*hire*

July *[leaf 148]*
2 at Congleton, in Cheshire
   at Ashton vnder Lyne, in Lanca-
    shire
11 at Partney, a horse fayre
   at Lid, in Kent
15 at Pinchback
17 at Winchcomb, in Glocester*shire*
20 at Vxbridge, in Midlesex
   at St Margrets, by Dartford
   at Catesby
   at Bolton, in Lancashire
22 On Mary Magdalens Day
   at Winchester
   at Marlborow
   at Colchester

at Tetbury.
at Bridgenorth.
at Clithero, in Lancashire.
at Northwich, in Cheshire.
at Keswik, in Cumberland.
at Battelfeild, by Shrewsbury.
25. On St. James Day.
   at Bristow.
   at Douer.
   at Chilham, in Kent.
   at Darby.
   at Ipswich.
   at Northampton.
   at Dudley.
   at St. James, by London.
   at Reading.
   at Lowth.
   at Malmsbury.
   at Bromley, in Kent.
   at Lirpoole, in Lancashire.
   at Altrincham, in Cheshire.
   at Rauenglas, in Cumberland.
27. at Canterbury.
   at Horsham, in Sussex.
   at Richmond.
   at Warrington, in Lancashire.
   at Chapellfirth, in Darbyshire.

[1486.]

August.

1 On Lammas Day.
   at Excester.
   at Brerton, in Cheshire.
   at Feuersham.
   at Dunstable.
   at St. Edes.
   at Bedford.
   at Norham Church.
   at Wisbich.
   at York.
   at Rumney.
   at Newton, in Lancashire.
   at Yeland, in Yorkshire.
10 On St. Laurence Day.
   at Waltham.
   at Blackmore.
   at Hungerford.
   at Bedford.
   at Stroud, in Kent.
   at Farnham, in Surrey.
   at St. Laurence, by Bodman.
   at Walton.
   at Crowley, in Lancashire.
   at Settell, in Yorkshire.
   at Frodsham, in Cheshire.
   at Mereworth, in Kent.
15. at Dunmow, in Essex.

at Carlile.
at Preston, in Aundernes.
at Wakefeld, the 2 Lady Dais.
24. at London.
   at Beggers Bush, besydes Rye.
   at Tewkesbury.
   at Sudbury.
   at Norwich.
   at Otford, in Kent.
   at Northalerton.
   at Douer.
   at Rye.
   at Crowley, in Lancashire.
   at Nantwich, in Cheshire.
28. at Ashford, in Kent.
Sonday after Bartelmew Day.
   at Sandbach, in Cheshire. This
   is now altered, for Sandbach hath
   2 fayres, to say, Tewsday &
   Wensday in Easter weke; &
   Thursday & Fryday beffore the
   Nativity of our Lady.

September. *[leaf 149.]

1. at St. Gyles, at the Bush.
8 On the nativytie of our Lady.
   at Wakefeld.
   at Sturbridge.
   at Southwark.
   at Snyde.
   at Recolvers, in Kent.
   at Gisborow, both the Lady Dais
   at Partney, the 3 Lady Daies.
   at Blackborn, in Lancashire.
   at Gisborn, in Yorkshyre.
   at Halton, in Cheshire.
   at Vteeter, in Staffordshire.
14. at Richmond.
   at Rippon, a horse fayre.
   at Penhead.
   at Berseley.
   at Waltham Abbay.
   at Wotton vnder Hedge, in Glo-
     cestershire.
   at Smalding.
   at Chesterfeld, in Darbyshire.
   at Denbigh.
17. at Cliff, in Kent.
21. at Marlborow.
   at Bedford.
   at Croidon.
   at Hedon, in Holdernes.
   at St. Edmunds Bury.
   at Malton.
   at St. Ives.
   at Shrewsbury.

	at Laneham	23	at Preston
	at Wiltnall		at Bickelsworth
	at Sittingborn, in Kent		at Ratchdale, in Lancashire
	at Bramtre, in Essex		at Low Knutsford, in Cheshire
	at New Brainford		at Whitchurch, in Shropshire
	at Katherin Hill, by Gilford	31	at Wakefeld
	at Douer		at Ruthin
	at Est Rye		
	at Canterbury		*November* *[leaf 150]*
29	at Chester	2	at Blechingligh
	at Lancaster		at Kingston
	at Blackborne, in Lancashire		at Maxfeld, in Cheshire
	at Cokermouth	6	at Newport Pond, in Essex
	at Ashborn, in Darbyshire		at Stanley
	at Hadley		at Tregni, in Cornwall
	at Maldon, a horse fayre		at Salford
	at Way Hill		at Lesford, in Lancashire
	at Newbery	10	at Lenton
	at Lecester	11	at Marlborow
			at Douer
	October.	13	at St Edmunds Bury
4	at Michell		at Gilford
6	at St Faiths, by Norwich	17	at Harlow
	at Maidston		at Hyde
8	at Herborow, in Lecestershire	19	at Horsham
	at Harnard	20	at Hith
	at Bishopstratford		at Engerston
11	at Croxston, in Lancashire	23	at Sandwich
	at Gravesend	30	at Colingborow
	at Windsor		at Rochester
	at Marchfeld		at Petersfeld
	at Colchester		at Maidenhead, in Barkshire
18	at Ely		at Bewdley, in Worcestershire
	at Wrickle		at Warrington, in Lancashire
	at Vpane		at Bareford, in Yorkshire
	at Thrusk		at Oswestry, in Shropshire
	at Bridgenorth		
	at Stanton		*December*
13	at Charing, in Kent	5	at Pluckley, in Kent
18	at Burton Appon Trent	6	On St Nicholas Day
	at Charlton, in Kent		at Spalding, in Lincolnshire
	at Wigan, in Lancashire		at Lecester
	at Friswides in Oxfordshire		at Sennock, in Kent
	at Tisdale, in Darbyshire		at Arndale
	at Midlewich in Cheshire		at Northwich, in Cheshire
	at Holt, in Denbighshire	7	at Sandherst, in Kent
21	at Safron Walden	8	On *the* Conception of *our* Lady
	at Newmarket		at Clithero, in Lancashire.
	at Hartford		at Malpas, in Cheshire
	at Ciceter, in Glocestershire	29	at Canterbury
	at Stokesley, in Yorkshire		at Salesbury

THE HIGH WAIS, FROM ANY NOTABLE TOWNE IN ENGLAND TO THE CITTIE OF LONDON, AND LYKEWYSE FROM ONE NOTABLE TOWNE TO ANOTHER

FROM ST BURIEN, IN CORNWALL, TO EXCESTER, & SO TO LONDON

	MYLES
from St Burien, to the Mount	12
from the Mount to Truro	20
from Truro, to Bodman	20
from Bodman, to Launston	12
from Launston, to Okhampton	15
from Okhampton, to Crokhornwell	10
from Crokenwell, to Excester	10
from Excester, to Honiton	12
from Honiton, to Chard	10
from Chard, to Crokhorn	6
from Crokehorne, to Sherborn	10
from Sherborne, to Shaftesbury	12
from Shaftesbury, to Salesbury	18
from Salesbury, to Andouer	15
from Andouer, to Basingstoke	16
from Basingstoke, to Hartlerow	8
from Hartlerow, to Bagshot	8
from Bagshot, to Stanes	8
from Stanes, to London	15
	237

*There is another way from Excester to London, and in maner as now, which some accompt the better way, and that is

from Excester, to Honiton	12
from Honiton, to Burport	16
from Burport, to Dorchester	12
from Dorchester, to Blandford	12
from Blandford to Salesbury	20

and so from Salesbury to London, as before

FROM TOTNES, TO EXCESTER

from Totnes, to Newton Bushell	8
from Newton Bushell, to Excester	12
	20

FROM PLIMOUTH, TO EXCESTER

from Plimouth, to Plimton	3
from Plimton, to Ashburton	16
from Ashburton, to Chidley	8
from Chidley, to Excester	8
	35

FROM DARTMOUTH, TO EXCESTER

from Dartmouth, pass the ferry, to Kingswere	
from Kingswere, to Cumpton	6
from Cumpton, to Newton Bushell	6

from Newton Bushell, to Excester	MYLES 12
	24

FROM EXCESTER, TO BARSTABLE

from Excester, to Crediton	7
from Crediton, to Copleston	3
from Copleston, to Coulridge	6
from Coulridge, to High Beckington	8
from High Beckington, to Barstable	6
	30

FROM EXCESTER, TO BRISTOW

from Excester, to Columpton	10
from Columton, to Wellington	8
from Wellington, to Taunton	5
from Taunton, to Bridgewater	7
from Bridge-water, to Glassenbury	11
from Glassonbury, to Welles	4
from Welles, to Bristow	15
	60

There is another way from Excester, to Bristow, and nere by 5 miles, which is from Bridge-water, through Brentmarsh, to Were, or Axbridge, & so to Bristow. But no man can trauell it well, except it be in somer tyme, or ells when it is a great frost.

FROM SOUTHAMPTON, TO HELFORD, IN CORNWALL, ALL ALONG THE SEA COAST

from Southampton, to Ringwood	12
from Ringwood, to Poole	8
from Poole, to Milton	15
from Milton, pass the ferry, to Waymouth	
from Waymouth, to Lyme	18
from Lyme, to Exmouth	15
from Exmouth, pass the ferry, to Tingmouth	10
from Tingmouth, pass the ferry, to Dartmouth	12
from Dartmouth, pass the ferry, to Salcomb	8
from Salcomb, take a guyde to Plimouth	14
from Plimouth, pass the ferry, to Saltash	3
from Saltash, to Low	10
from Low, to Foy	8
from Foy, pass the ferry, to Truro	18
from Truro, to Helford	6

FROM SOUTHAMPTON, TO BRISTOW

	MYLES
from Southampton, to Salesbury	18
from Salesbury, to Warmister	18
from Warmister to Bath	14
from Bath, to Bristow	10
	60

FROM SOUTHAMPTON, TO LONDON [leaf 152]

from Southampton to Twiford	8
from Twiford, to Alesford	7
from Alesford, to Alton	7
from Alton, to Farnham	6
from Farnham to Gilford	7
from Gilford to Ripley	5
from Ripley, to Coucham	5
from Coucham to Kingston	5
from Kingston to Wansworth	5
from Wansworth, to London	5
	60

FROM BARSTABLE, TO BRISTOW

from Barstable, to Dunster	18
from Dunster, to Comidge	12
from Comage, to Weare	10
from Weare, to Bristow	15
	55

FROM BRISTOW, TO OXFORD

from Bristow, to Sodbury	10
from Sodbury, to Cicetcr	12
from Cicetcr, to Faringdon	14
from Faringdon, to Oxford	12
	48

*FROM BRISTOW, TO SHREWSBURY [leaf 153]

from Bristow to Aust	8
from Aust, pass *the* ferry, to Betesley	1
from Betesley to Monmouth	11
from Monmouth, to Hereford	12
from Hereford, to Lemster	8
from Lemster to Ludlow	7
from Ludlow, to Shrewsbury	20
	67

ANOTHER WAY FROM BRISTOW, TO SHREWSBURY, AND SO TO CHESTER

from Bristow, to Glocester	30
from Glocester to Tewkesbury	7
from Tewkesbury, to Worcester	13
from Worcester to Kiddermister	10
from Kiddermister to Bridgenorth	12
from Bridgenorth, to Shrewsbury	14
from Shrewsbury, to Chester	30
	116

FROM BRISTOW, TO CAMBRIDGE

	MYLES
from Bristow, to Sodbury	10
from Sodbury, to Cicetcr	12
from Cicetcr, to Burford	10
from Burford, to Woodstock	15
from Woodstock, to Buckingham	15
from Buckingham, to Newport Panell	10
from Newport Panell, to Bedford	10
from Bedford to Gransden	10
from Gransden, to Cambridge	10
	97

*FROM BRISTOW TO LONDON [leaf 153b]

from Bristow to Marsfeld	10
from Marsfeld to Chippenham	10
from Chippenham, to Calne	4
from Calne, to Marlborow	10
from Marlborow, to Hungerford	8
from Hungerford, to Newbery	7
from Newbery, to Reding	15
from Reding, to Maidenhead	10
from Maidenhead, to Colbroke	7
from Colbroke, to Bramford	8
from Bramford, to London	8
	97

FROM YORK, TO NOTTINGHAM

from York, to Tadcaster	8
from Tadcaster, to Wentbridge	12
from Wentbridge, to Doncaster	7
from Doncaster to Maunsfeld	20
from Maunsfeld to Nottingham	12
	59

FROM YORK, TO CAMBRIDGE

from York, kepe London way, untill you come to Huntington, and then you have 12 myles to Cambridge

*FROM BARWIK, TO YORK, & SO TO LONDON [leaf 154]

from Barwik, to Belford	12
from Belford, to Alnwick	12
from Alnwick, to Morpith	12
from Morpith to Newcastell	12
from Newcastell, to Durham	12
from Durham, to Darrington	14
from Darrington, to Northalerton	10
from North-Alerton, to Topcliff	7
from Topcliff, to York	16
from York, to Tadcaster	8
from Tadcaster, to Wentbridge	12
from Wentbridge to Doncaster	7
from Doncaster, to Tuxford	18
from Tuxford to Newark	10
from Newark, to Grantham	10
from Grantham, to Stamford	16

		MYLES
	from Stamford, to Stilton	12
	from Stilton, to Huntington	9
	from Huntington, to Roiston	15
	from Roiston, to Ware	13
	from Ware, to Waltham	8
	from Waltham, to London	12
		—
		258
af 1548]	*FROM YORK, TO CHESTER	
	from York, to Wetherby	7
	from Wetherby, to Oteley	13
	from Oteley, to Bradford	6
	from Bradford, to Halifax	6
	from Halifax, to Blackston Edge	6
	from Blackston Edge, to Rachdale	6
	from Rachdale, to Manchester	8
	from Manchester, to Northwich	16
	from Northwich, to Chester	12
		—
		80
	FROM YORK, TO SHREWSBURY	
	kepe Chester way as beffore, untill you come to Northwich, which is	68
	from Northwich, to Beeston Castell	9
	from Beston, to Whitchurch	10
	from Whitchurch, to Prees	4
	from Prees, to Shrewsbury	12
		—
		103
	FROM LINCOLNE, TO LONDON	
	from Lincolne, to Ancaster	16
	from Ancaster, to Bichfeld	8
	from Bichfeld, to Stamford	12
	and so from Stamford, to London, as beffore	69
		—
		105
eaf 155]	*FROM BOSTON, TO LONDON	
	from Boston, to Donington	10
	from Donington, to Borne	12
	from Borne, to Stilton	18
	and so from Stilton to London, as beffore	57
		—
		97
	FROM ST DAUIDS, IN WALES, LONDON	10
	from St Dauids, to Harford	12
	from Harford, to Carmarden	24
	from Carmarden, to Newton	12
	from Newton, Lanbury	10
	from Lanbury, to Brecknock	16
	from Brecknock, to Hay	10
	from Hay, to Hereford	14
	from Hereford, to Ross	9
	from Ross, to Glocester	12

		MYLES
	from Glocester, to Cicceter	15
	from Cicceter, to Faringdon	12
	from Faringdon, to Abbington	10
	from Abbington, to Dorchester	5
	from Dorchester, to Henley	12
	from Henley, to Maidenhead	7
	from Maidenhead, to Colbrok	7
	from Colbrok, to London	16
		—
		203
	*FROM WORCESTER, TO LONDON	*[leaf 155]
	from Worcester, to Euesham	12
	from Euesham, to Chipping Norton	13
	from Chipping-Norton, to Ishpp	12
	from Ishpp, to High Wickam	20
	from High-Wickam, to Beconsfeld	5
	from Beconsfeld, to Uxbridge	7
	from Uxbridge, to London	15
		—
		84
	FROM CARNARUAN, TO CHESTER, & so TO LONDON	
	from Carnaruan, to Conway	24
	from Conway, to Denbigh	12
	from Denbigh, to Flint	12
	from Flint, to Chester	10
	from Chester, to Nantwich	14
	from Nantwich, to Stone	15
	from Stone, to Lichfeld	16
	from Lichfeld, to Colshill	12
	from Colshill, to Couentrie	8
	from Couentrie, to Daintree	14
	from Daintree, to Towcester	10
	from Towcester, to Stoniestretford	6
	from Stoniestretford, to Brickhill	7
	from Brickill, to Dunstable	7
	from Dunstable, to St Albones	10
	from St Albones, to Barnet	10
	from Barnet, to London	10
		—
		197
	*FROM CARLILE, TO LANCASTER, & so TO LONDON	*[leaf 156]
	from Carlile, to Keswik	18
	from Keswik, to Gresmere	8
	from Gresmere, to Kendall	14
	from Kendale, to Burton	7
	from Burton to Lancaster	8
	from Lancaster, to Preston	20
	from Preston, to Wigan	14
	from Wigan, to Warrington	12
	from Warrington, to Hulmes Chapell	12
	from Hulmes Chapell, to Newcastell	10
	from Newcastell, to Stone	4
	from Stone, to Lichfeld	16
	from Lichfeld, to Couentrie	20

	MYLES
and so from Couentry, to London, as beffore	74
	237
FROM SHREWSBURY, TO LONDON	
from Shrewsbury, to Wathngstreet	7
from Wathngstreet to Shifnall	5
from Shifnall, to Wollerhampton	8
from Wollerhampton, to Bermicham	10
from Bermincham, to Meriden	10
from Meriden, to Couentrye	4
and so from Coventry, to London, as beffore	74
	118

[leaf 156*] *FROM COUENTRY TO OXFORD
from Couentrie, to Southam	10
from Southam, to Banbury	10
from Banbury, to Woodstock	12
from Woodstock, to Oxford	7
	39

FROM COUENTRY, TO CAMBRIDGE
from Couentry, to Dunchurch	8
from Dunchurch, to Northampton	10
from Northampton, to Higham Ferries	10
from Higham Ferries, to St Edes	8
from St Edes, to Cambridge	10
	46

FROM CAMBRIDGE, TO LONDON
from Cambridge, to Slow	6
from Slow to Barkway	7
from Barkway to Ware	12
from Ware to Waltham	8
from Waltham, to London	12
	45

FROM OXFORD, TO LONDON
from Oxford, to Tetsworth	10
from Tetsworth, to Wickam	10
from Wickam, to Beconsfeld	5
from Beconsfeld to Vxbridge	7
from Vxbridge, to London	15
	47

[leaf 157] *FROM DOUER TO LONDON
from Douer, to Canterbury	12
from Canterbury to Sittingborne	12
from Sittingborn, to Rochester	8
from Rochester to Gravesend	5

	MYLES
from Grauesend, to Dartford	6
from Dartford, to London	12
	55

FROM RYE, TO LONDON
from Rye, to Plimwell	15
from Plimwell, to Tunbridge	11
from Tunbridge, to Chepstow	7
from Chepstow, to London	15
	48

FROM YERMOUTH, TO COLCHESTER, & SO TO LONDON
from Yermouth, to Lestoff	6
from Lestoff, to Bliborow	10
from Bliborow, to Snape Bridge	8
from Snape Bridge, to Woodbridge	8
from Woodbridge, to Ipswich	5
from Ipswich, to Colchester	12
from Colchester, to Esterford	8
from Esterford, to Wittam	3
from Wittam, to Chelmsford	7
from Chelmsford, to Brentwood	10
from Brentwood, to London	15
	92

*FROM WALSINGHAM, TO LONDON   *[leaf 157b]
from Walsingham, to Picknam	12
from Picknam, to Brandon Ferry	10
from Brandon Ferry, to Newmarket	10
from Newmarket, to Witford Bridge	10
from Witford Bridge to Barkway	12
from Barkway, to Ware	12
from Ware, to London	20
	86

FROM YERMOUTH, TO NORWICH
from Yermouth, to Ockell	8
from Ockell, to Norwich	8
	16

FROM NORWICH, TO LONDON
from Norwich, to Windham	6
from Windham, to Atlebury	4
from Atlebury, to Thetford	10
from Thetford, to Icklingham	6
from Icklingham, to Newmarket	10
from Newmarket to Barkway	22
and so from Barway to London, as beffore	32
	90

[1] So in the MS

FINIS

[leaf 158a contains shields of the author's Arms, and of his family connections see Plate XVII]

PLATE I.

Dover. Hastings. Bedford. Northampton.

Kingston. Southampton. Buckingham. Hereford.

Exeter. Ipswich. Worcester. Warwick.

London.

Duchy of Lancaster.

PLATE II.

Leicester. Bishopric of Durham. York. Isle of Man. Durham. Lincoln. Newcastle. Nottingham. Shrewsbury. Lancaster. Cheshire. York.

Yorkshire.

PLATE III.

ARCHBISHOPS AND BISHOPS.

CANTERBURY. YORK.

London. Winchester. Norwich. Ely.

Worcester. Salisbury. Lincoln. Hereford.

Lichfield & Coventry. Chichester. Bath & Wells. Exeter.

Peterborough. Rochester. Gloucester. Bristol.

PLATE IV.

BISHOPS.

Oxford. St David. St Asaph. Llandaff.

Bangor. Durham. Chester. Carlisle.

EARLS OF PEMBROKE.

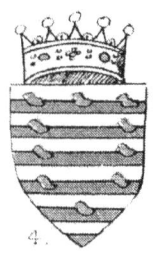

1. 2. 3. 4. 5.

6. 7. 8. 9. 10.

PLATE V

EARLS OF KENT.

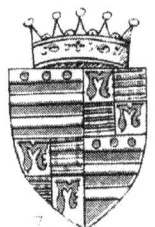

NORTHUMBERLAND.

LEICESTER

PLATE VI.

SURREY

EARLS OF WARWICK

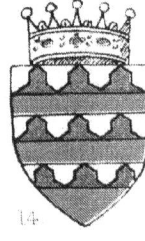

PLATE VII.

PLATE VIII.

WALES AND CHESTER.

EARLS OF WINCHESTER.

PLATE IX.

EARLS OF LINCOLN

WORCESTER

EARLS OF WILTSHIRE

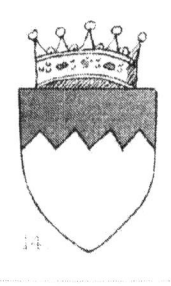

PLATE X.

EARLS OF ESSEX.

EARLS OF NORTHAMPTON.

EARLS OF SALISBURY.

PLATE XI

EARLS OF DEVONSHIRE.

DORSET.

HEREFORD.

EARLS OF CARLISLE.

SHREWSBURY.

OXFORD.

PLATE XII.

SOMERSET.

HUNTINGDON.

DUKES OF NORFOLK.

PLATE XIII.

CAMBRIDGE.

STAFFORD.

BUCKINGHAM.

EXETER.

EARL OF BATH.

WESTMORELAND.

NORWICH.

PLATE XIV.

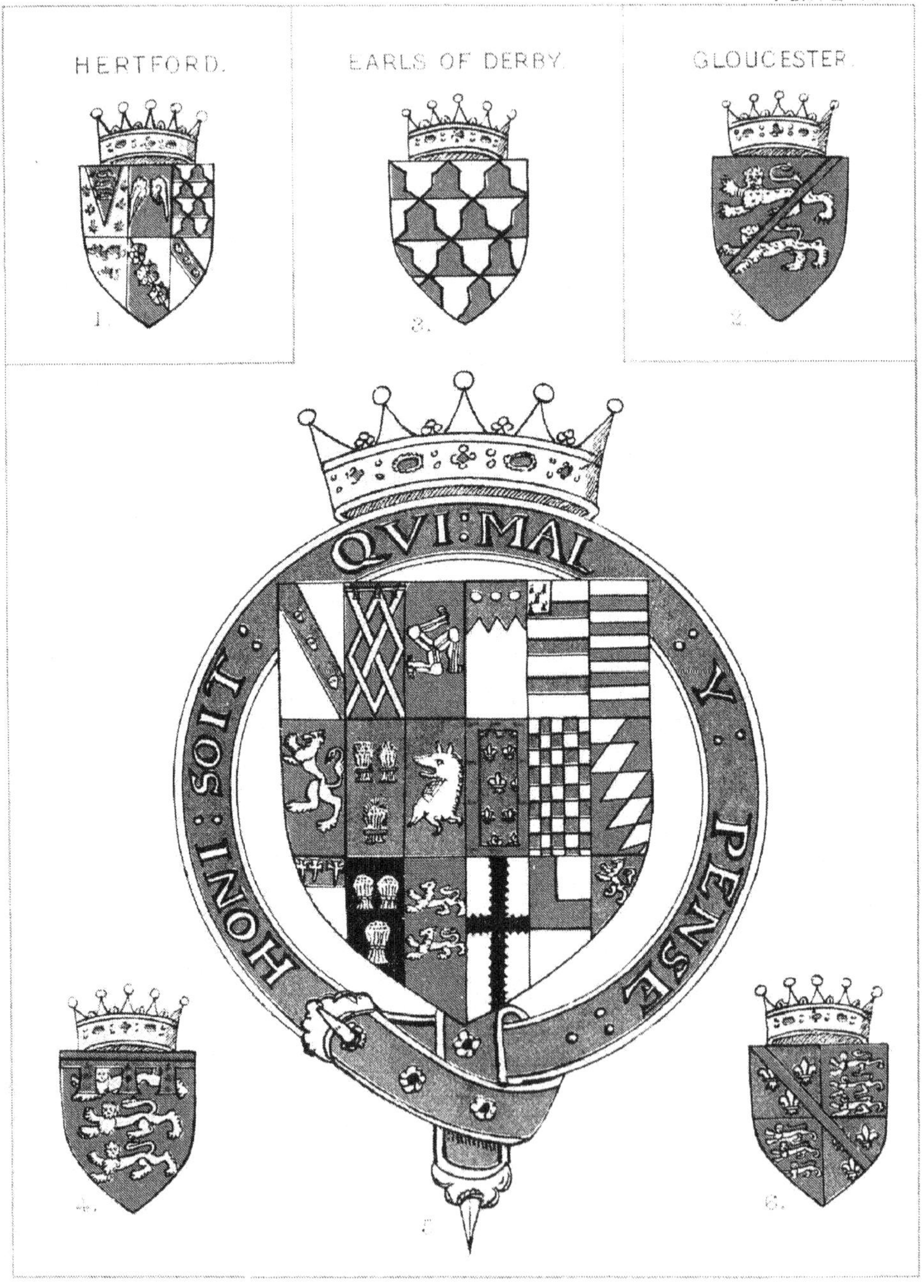
HERTFORD.
EARLS OF DERBY.
GLOUCESTER.
1.
3.
2.
QVI:MAL
HONI : SOIT
Y PENSE
4.
5.
6.

PLATE XV.

EARLS OF GLOUCESTER

SUFFOLK.

PLATE XVI.

EARLS OF NOTTINGHAM.

CUMBERLAND.

EARLS OF RUTLAND.

YORKSHIRE.

PLATE XVII.

SILENTIO ET SPE.

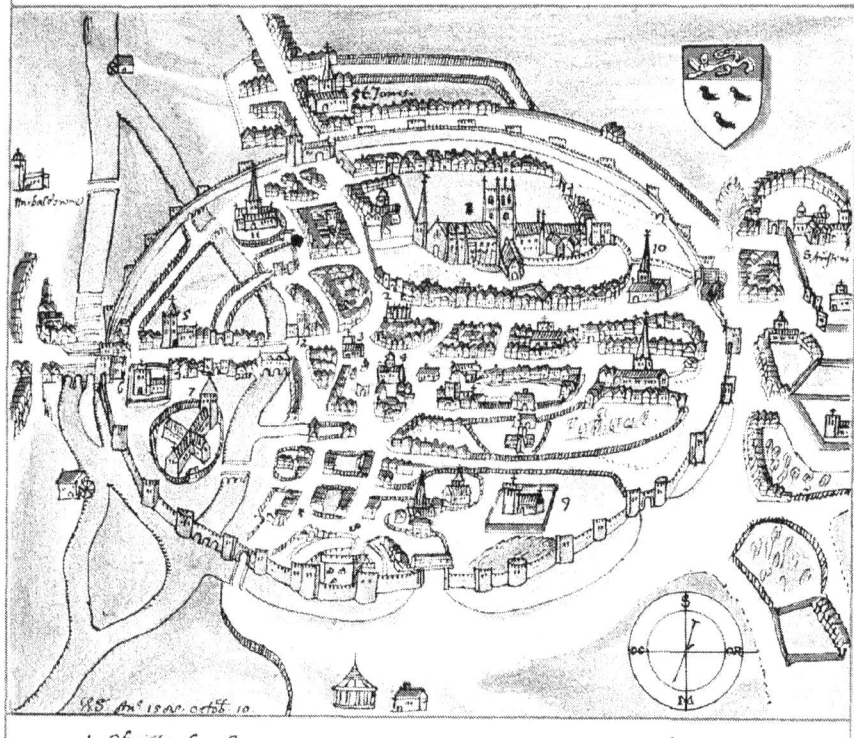

PLATE XVIII.

PLATE XIX.

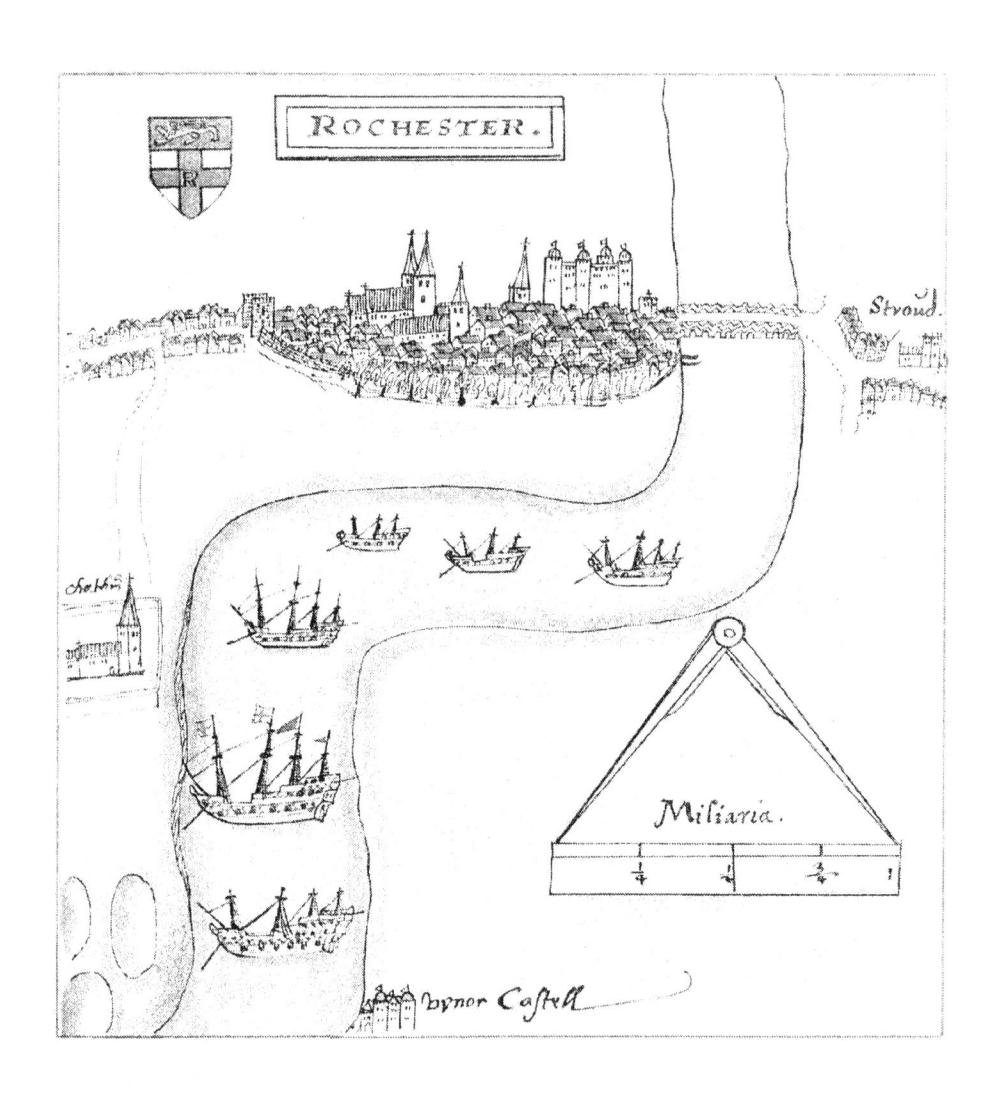

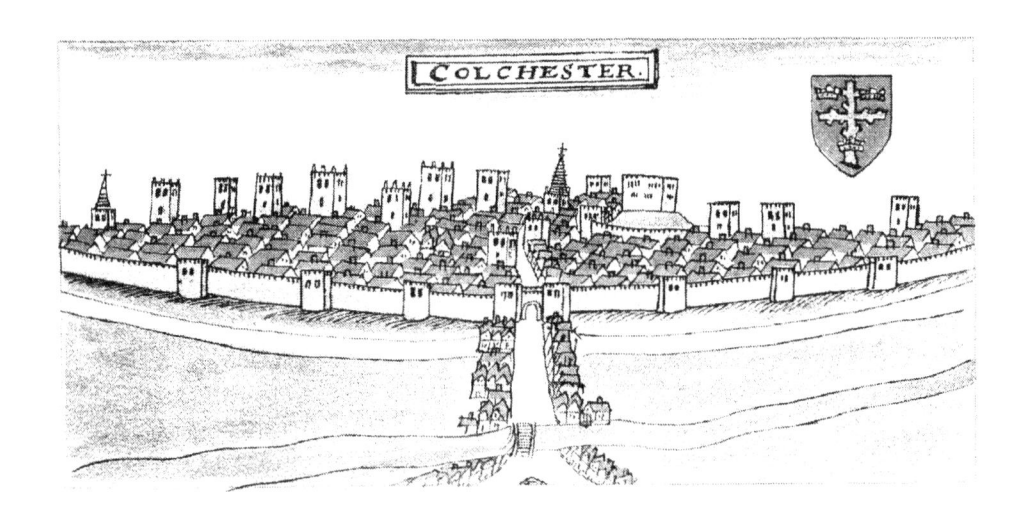

PLATE XX.

PLATE XXI.

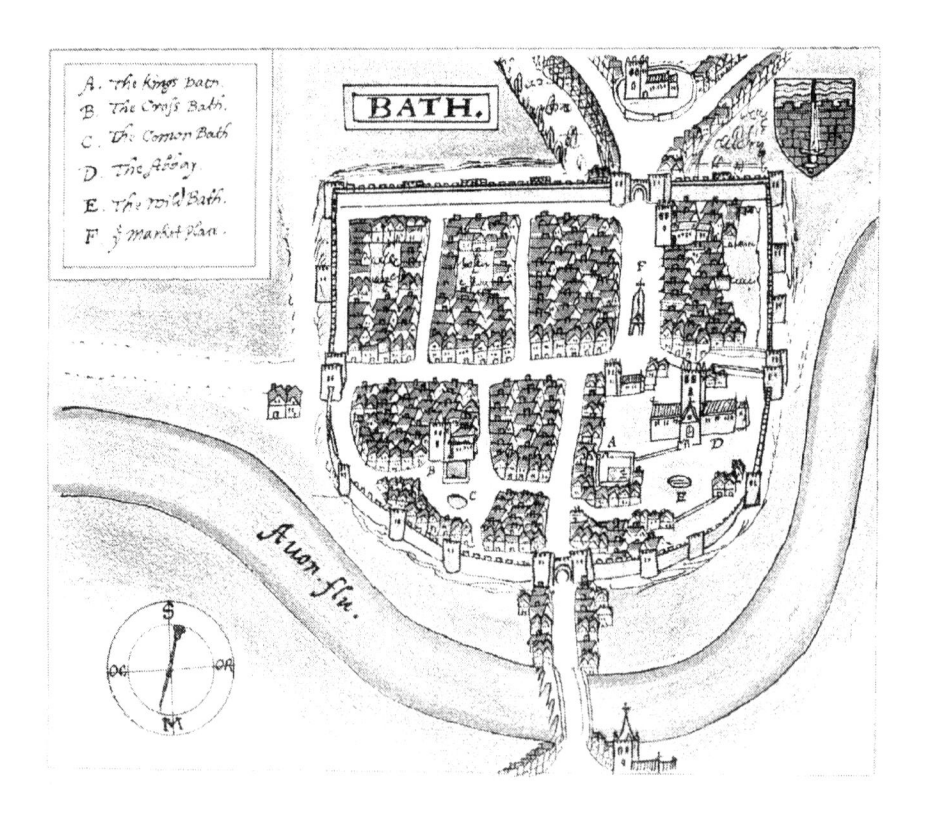

PLATE XXII

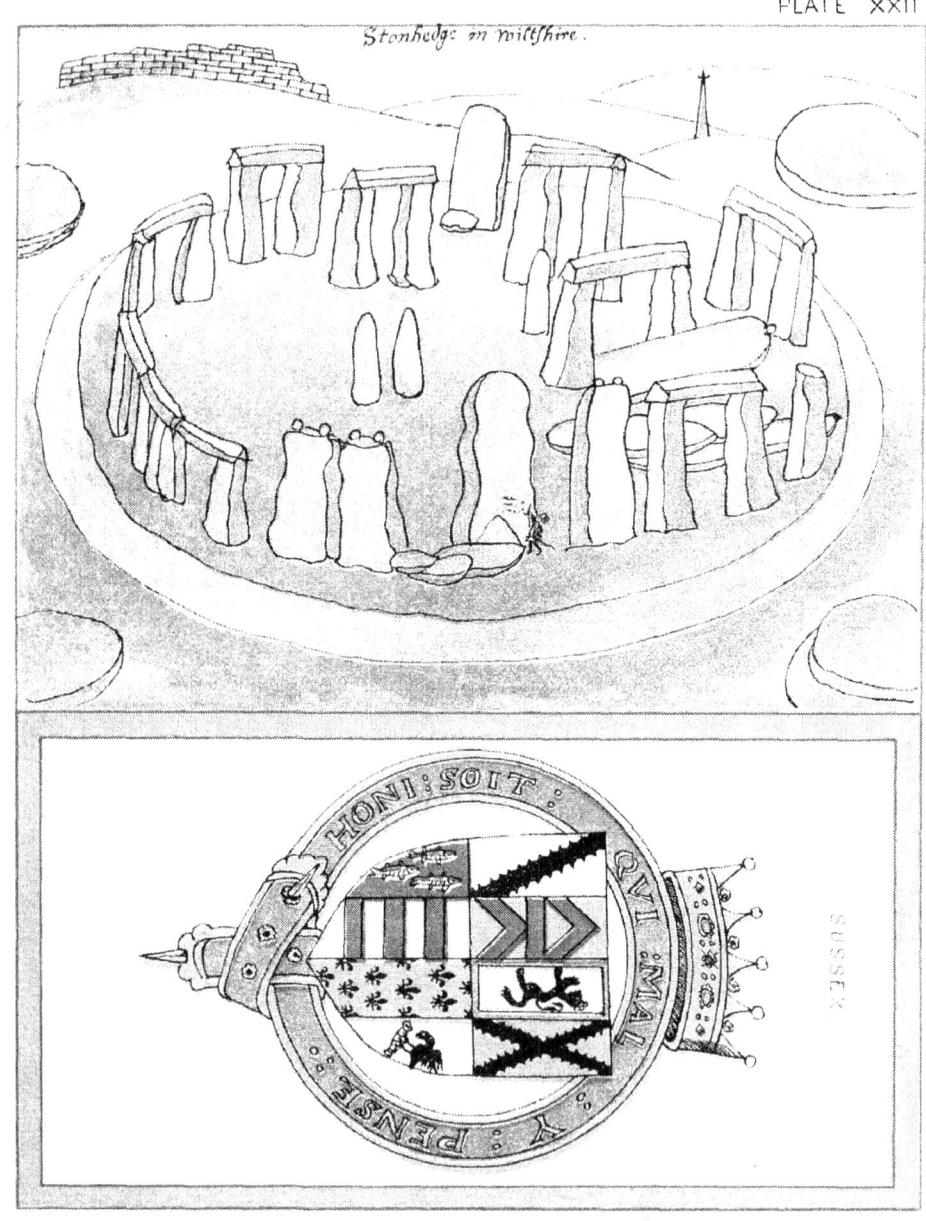

Stonhedge in Wiltshire.

PLATE XXIII

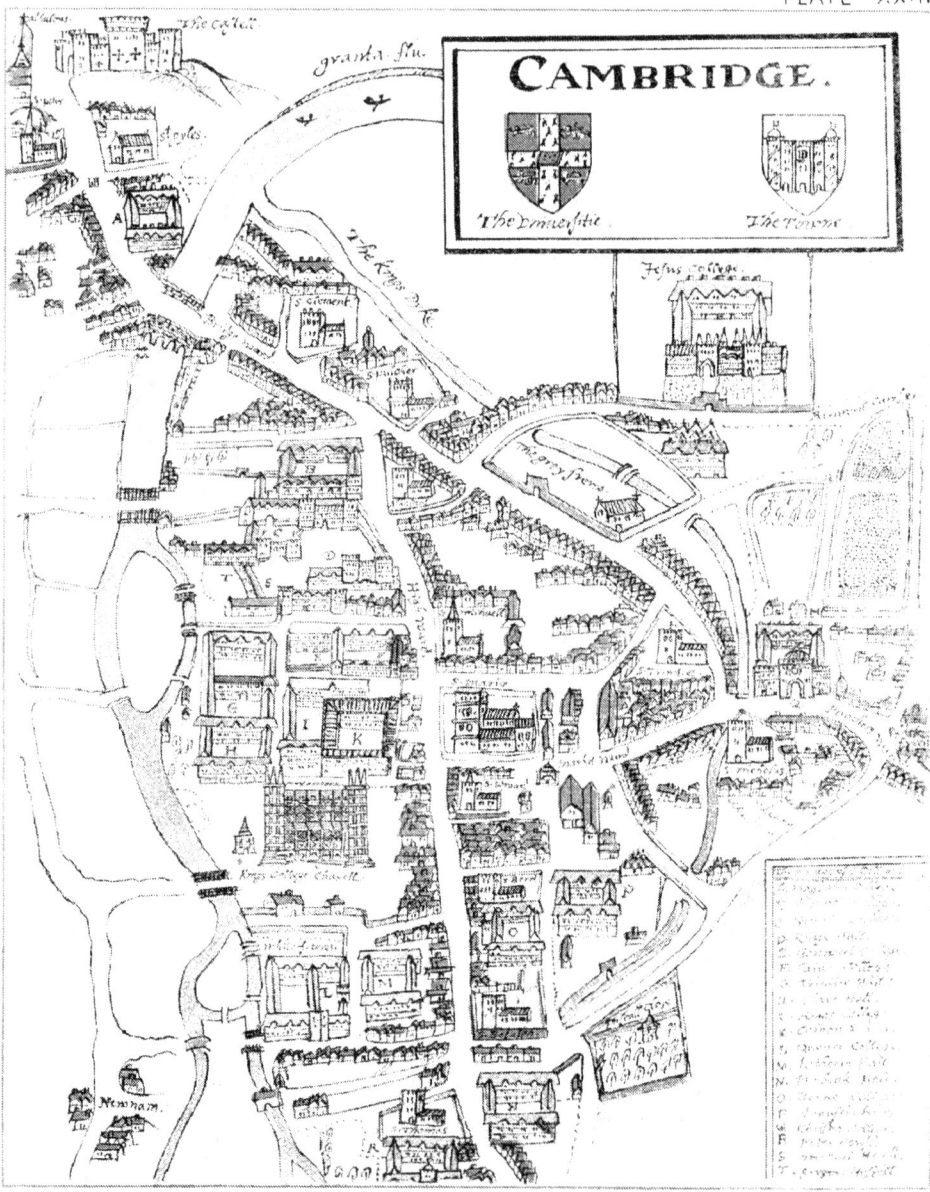

PLATE XXIV.

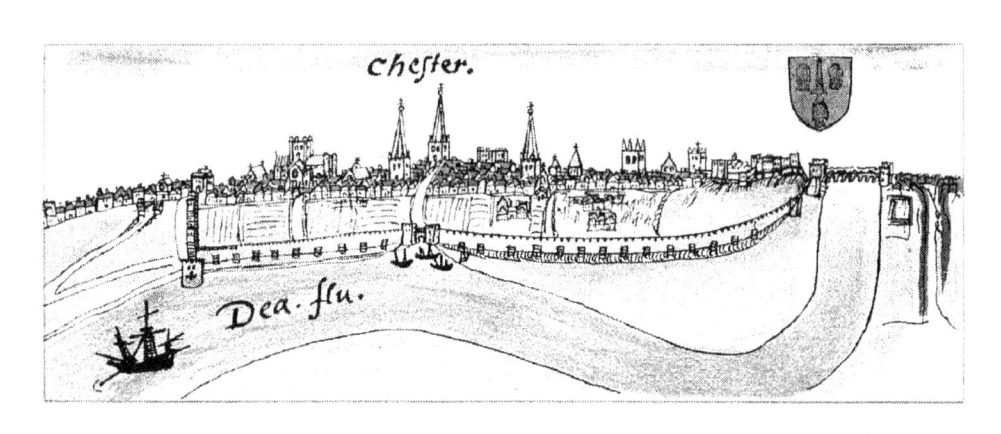

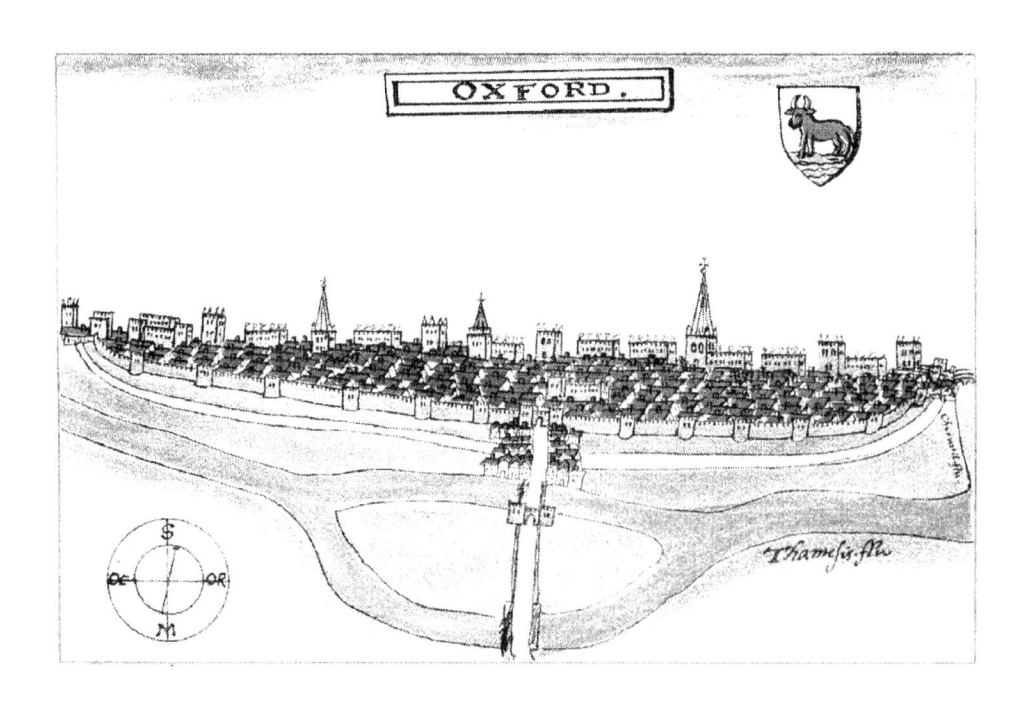

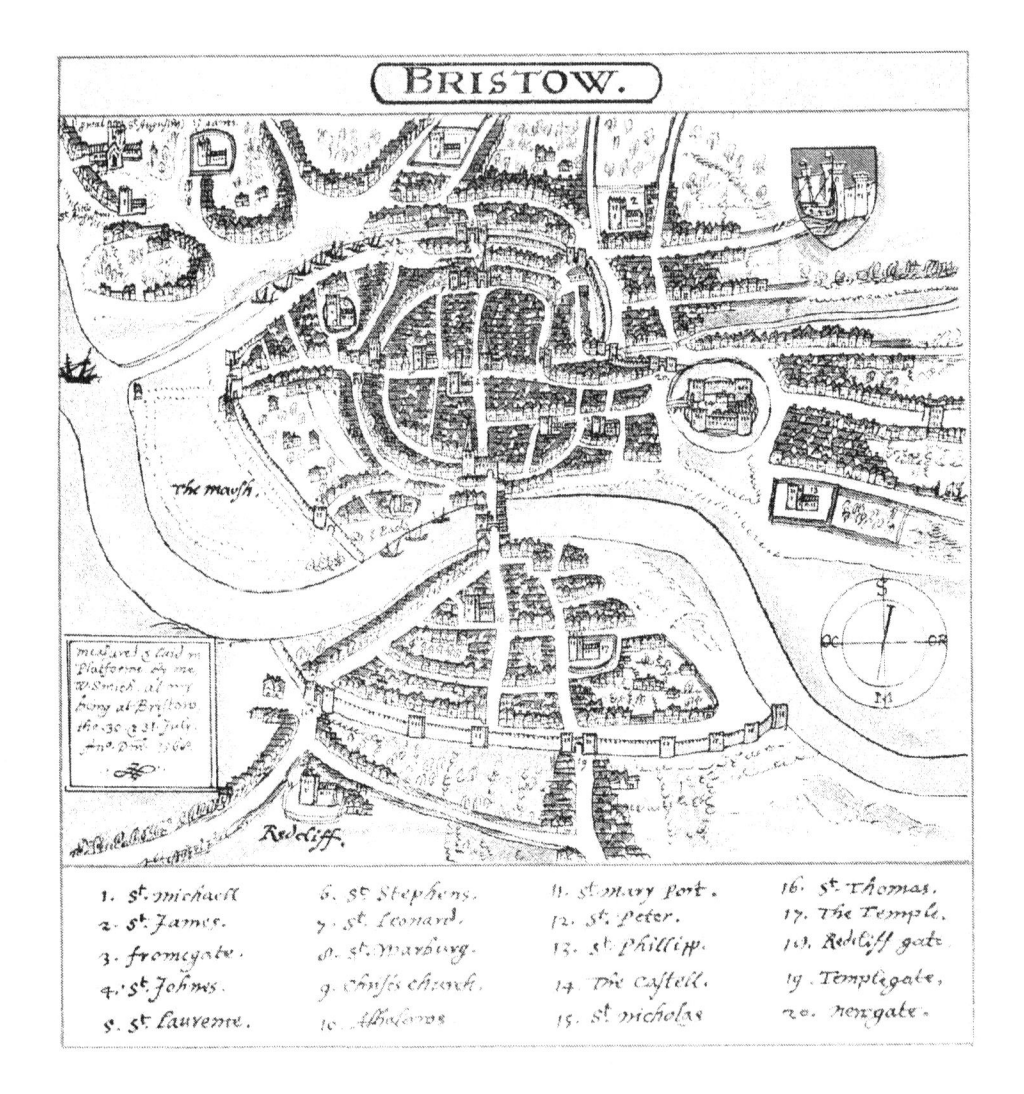

PLATE XXV.

BRISTOW.

1. St. Michaell
2. St. James.
3. Fromegate.
4. St. Johnes.
5. St. Laurence.
6. St. Stephens.
7. St. Leonard.
8. St. Warburg.
9. Christs Church.
10. Allhalows.
11. St. Mary port.
12. St. Peter.
13. St. Phillipp.
14. The Castell.
15. St. Nicholas.
16. St. Thomas.
17. The Temple.
18. Redcliff gate.
19. Templegate.
20. Newgate.

PLATE XXVI.

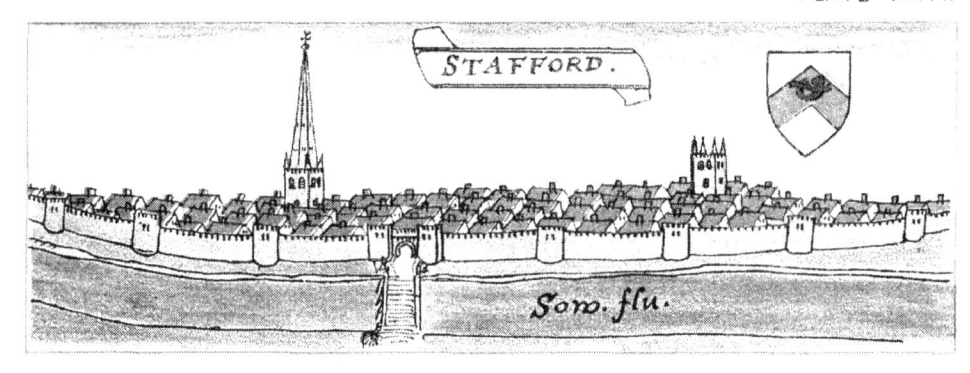

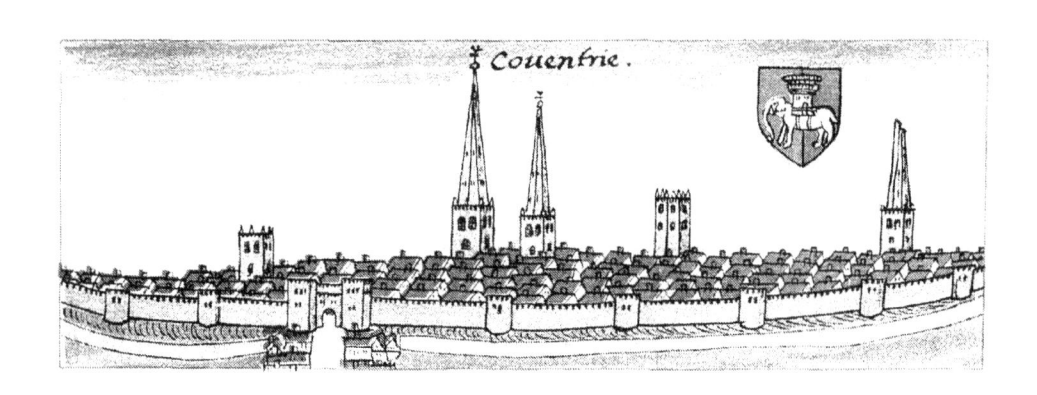

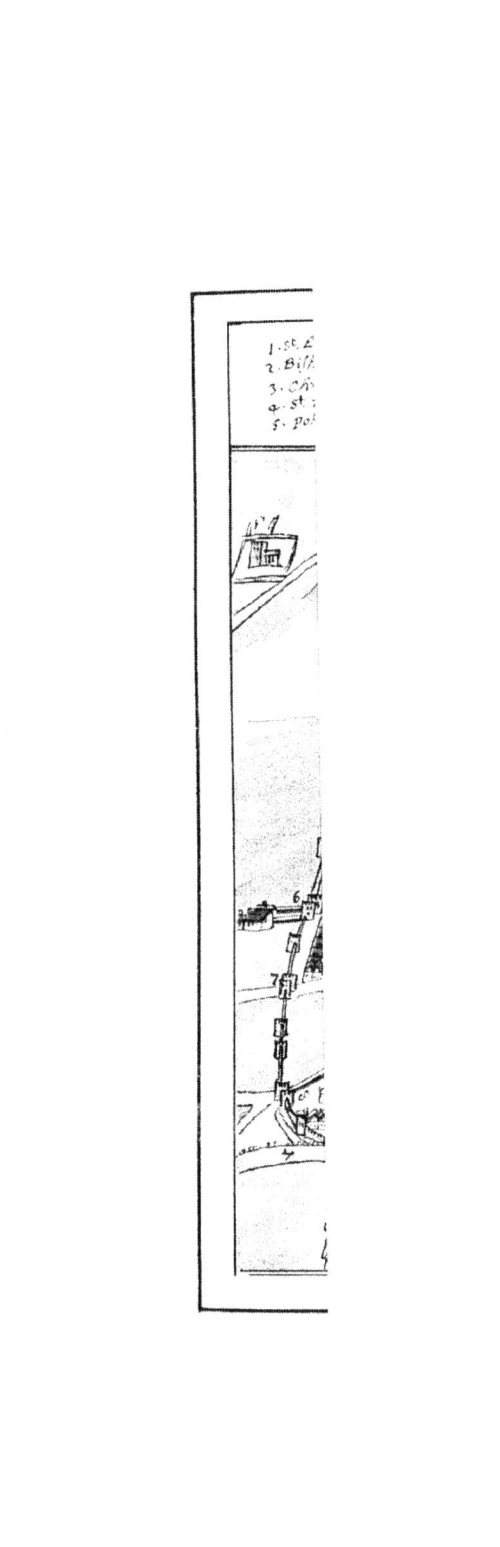

PLATE XXVII.

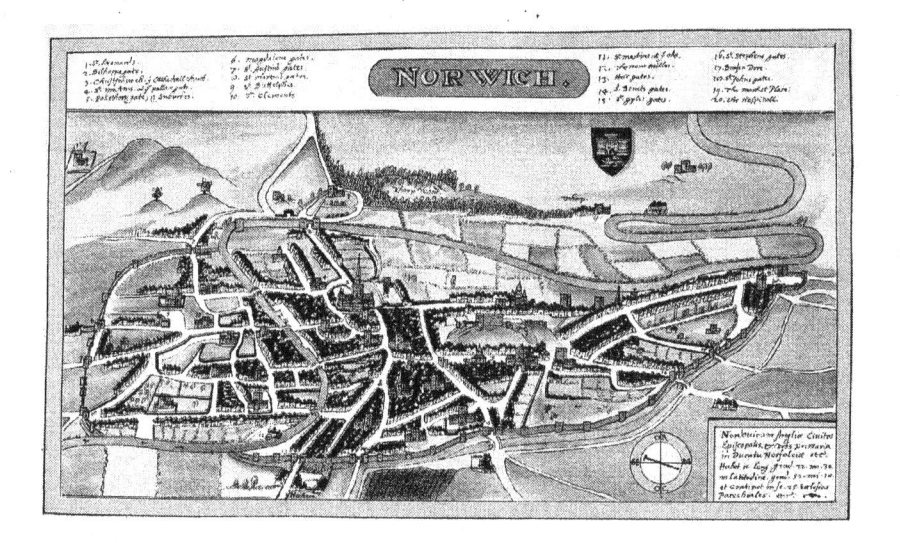

PLATE XXVIII.

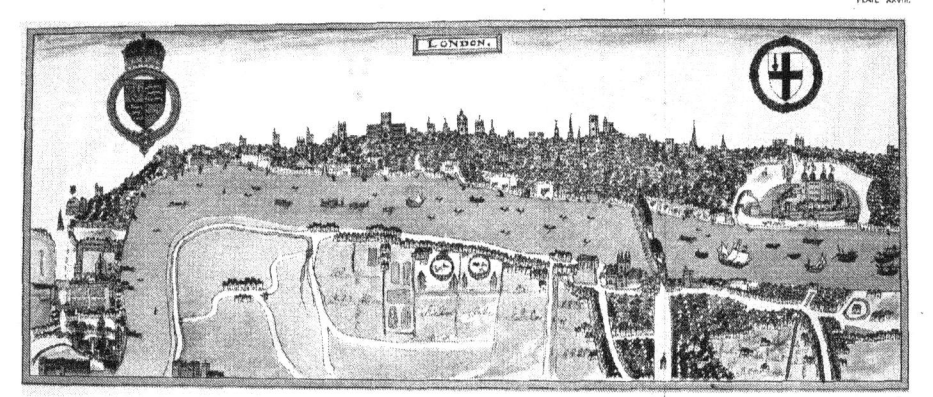

LONDON.

PLATE XXVIII.

INDEX.

Abbeys which sometime were in Yorkshire, p 50
Agas (Ralph), his view of Cambridge, ix
Altensteig, Arms of, Plate XVII
Altensteig (Francis), father-in-law of William Smith, vi
Anglesea, 58-59, Castles, 59
Archbishops, Arms of, Plate III
Arms (College of), William Smith becomes an officer of, vii
Arundel (Earls of), Arms of, Plates VI, XI
Aumale (Duke of), Arms of, Plate XVI

Barkshire, 14-15
Bath, View of, Plate XXI
Bath (Earls of), Arms of, Plate XIII
Bedford, Arms of, Plate I
Bedford (Baron, Earl and Duke of), Arms of, Plates IV, VII
Berkshire, 14-15
Bishoprics in England, 4
Bishops, Arms of, Plates III, IV
Bond (E A), Principal Librarian of the British Museum, x
Bostock, Arms of, Plate XVII
Bostock (Ralph), of Norcroft, grandfather of William Smith, vi
Brecknockshire, 55, Castles, 55
Bristol, View of, vi, viii, Plate XXV
Bristow and Cornwall (Earl of), Arms of, Plates VII, XIV
Brittain (Earl of), Arms of, Plate XVI
Buckingham, Arms of, Plate I
Buckingham (Earls and Dukes of), Arms of, Plate XIII
Buckinghamshire 32, Forests in, 33
Burgesses of the Parliament, x, 62-64

Cambridge, View of, ix, Plate XXIII
Cambridge (Earls of), Arms of, Plate XIII
Cambridgeshire, 29-30
Canterbury, View of, Plate XVIII
Cardiganshire, 56-57, Forests, 57
Carlisle (Earls of), Arms of, Plate XI
Carmardenshire, 55, Forests, 55, Castles, 56

Carnarvanshire, 58, Castles, 58
Castles in England —
 Cheshire, 46
 Cumberland, 52
 Darbyshire, 42
 Durham, 51
 Herefordshire, 36
 Kent, 9
 Lancashire, 47
 Northumberland, 53
 Shropshire, 44
 Staffordshire, 43
 Westmerland, 51
 Yorkshire, 50
 ———— in Wales
 Anglesea, 59
 Brecknockshire, 55
 Carmardenshire, 56
 Carnarvanshire, 58
 Denbighshire, 59
 Glamorganshire, 55
 Merinothshire, 58
 Monmouthshire, 54
 Montgomeryshire, 57
 Penbrokshire, 56
 Radnorshire, 57
Channel Islands, 60
Cheshire, 44-46, Forests, 46, Castles, 46
————, Arms of, Plate II
Chester, Sketch of, Plate XXIV
Chester (Earls of), Arms of, Plates VII, VIII
Clarence (Duke of), Arms of, Plate XVI
Colchester, Sketch of, Plate XX
Cornwall, 22-24
Cornwall (Earls and Dukes of) Arms of, Plate VII
Coventry, Sketch of, Plate XXVI
Crace Collection of London Maps *referred to*, ix
Cumberland, 51-52, Forests, 52, Castles, 52
Cumberland (Earls of), Arms of, Plate XVI

Darbyshire, 41, Forests, 42, Castles, 42
Denbighshire, 59, Castles, 59
Derby (Earls of), Arms of, Plate XIV

10

Derbyshire, 41-42
Dethick (Sir Gilbert), Garter King-at-Arms, vii, viii
Devon (Earl of), Arms of, Plate XIII
Devonshire, 20-22
Devonshire (Earls of), Arms of, Plate XI
Dorset (Marquesses of), Arms of, Plates XI, XIII
Dorsetshire, 17-18, Forests in, 18, Vales, 18
Dover, Arms of, Plate I
Durham, 50-51, Forests, 51, Castles, 51
———— Arms of, Plate II
———— (Bishopric of), Arms of, Plate II

England, How England took name, 1
———— A Description of, 2
———— Shyres in, 2-3
———— Bishopricks in, 4
———— Four Principall Rivers in, 4-5
———— Wonders in, ix, 6
———— Map of, *frontispiece*
Essex, 24-25, Forests in, 25
Essex (Earls of), Arms of, Plate X
Estalnge (Earl of), Arms of, Plate XIII
Exeter, Arms of, Plate I
Exeter (Marquis and Dukes of), Arms of, Plate XIII

Fairs kept in England, x, 65-68
Fhurer (Christopher), the *Angliæ Descriptio* dedicated to him, vi
Finden's (Anthony von) View of London, ix
Flintshire, 59, Castles, 59
Forests in England —
    Buckinghamshire, 33
    Cheshire, 46
    Cumberland, 52
    Darbyshire, 42
    Dorsetshire, 18
    Durham, 51
    Essex, 25
    Glocestershire, 35
    Hamshire, 13
    Herefordshire, 36
    Lancashire, 46
    Leicestershire, 38
    Northamptonshire, 32
    Nottinghamshire, 41
    Rutland, 39
    Shropshire, 44
    Somersetshire, 20
    Staffordshire, 43
    Sussex, 10-11
    Westmorland, 5
    Wiltshire, 16
    Worcestershire, 37
    Yorkshire, 56
    ———— in Wales
    Cardiganshire, 57
    Carmardenshire, 55
    Monmouthshire, 54

Penbrokshire, 56
Radnorshire, 57
Furnivall (F. J.), draws the editors' attention to Smith's MS, v
Glamorganshire, 54-55, Castles, 55
Gloucester (Earls and Dukes of), Arms of, Plates IV, XIII, XV
Gloucestershire, 34-35, Forests in, 35

Hamshire, 12-14
Harrison's Description of England *referred to* x
Hartfordshire, 26
Hastings, Arms of, Plate I
Hereford, Arms of, Plate I
Hereford (Viscount, Earls, and Duke of), Arms of, Plate XI
Herefordshire, 35-36, Forests, 36, Castles, 36
Hertford (Earl of), Arms of, Plate XIV
Hertfordshire, 26
Highways from any notable town in England to the city of London, and from one notable town to another, x, 62-72
Holy Island, or Lindisfarne, 61
Huntingdon (Earls of), Arms of, Plates XII, XIII
Huntingdonshire, 30-31.

Ipswich, Arms of, Plate I
Islands, 59-62

Kent, 6-9, Castles in, 9, Manor places belonging to the King, 9
Kent (Earls of), Arms of, Plate V
Kingston, Arms of, Plate I

Lancashire, 46-47, Forests, 47, Castles, 47
Lancaster, Arms of, Plate II
———— (Duchy of), Arms of, Plate I
Leicester, Arms of, Plate II
Leicester (Earls of), Arms of, Plate V
Leicestershire, 38, Forests, 38
Lichfield, Sketch of, Plate XXVI
Lincoln, Arms of, Plate II
Lincoln (Earls of), Arms of, Plate IX
Lincolnshire, 39-40
Lindisfarne or Holy Island, 61
London, Arms of, Plate I
———— View of, Plate XXVIII
Lundy Island, 61
Lyne's (Richard) View of Cambridge, ix

Man, Isle of, 61-62, Arms of, Plate II
Manor places belonging to the King—Kent, 9
Mermouthshire, 58, Castles, 58
Methuen (Sir Paul), possessor of the "Description of England," v
Middelsex, 25-26
Miles, difference between the reputed and measured, x

INDEX.

Monmouthshire, 53–54; Forests, 54; Castles, 54.
Montgomeryshire, 57; Castles, 57.
Moors in Somersetshire, 20.

Newcastle, Arms of, Plate II.
Noble's History of the College of Arms, *referred to* v, vii, viii.
Norfolk, 28–29.
Norfolk (Earl and Dukes of), Arms of, Plate XII.
Northampton, Arms of, Plate I.
Northampton (Earls and Marquess of), Arms of, Plates X., XII.
Northamptonshire, 31–32; Forests in, 32.
Northumberland, 52–53; Castles, 53.
Northumberland (Earls of), Arms of, Plates V., XII.
Norwich, View of, Plate XXVII.
Norwich (Earls of), Arms of, Plate XIII.
Nottingham, Arms of, Plate II.
Nottingham (Earls of), Arms of, Plate XVI.
Nottinghamshire, 40–41; Forest, 41.
Nuremberg, William Smith settled there for a time, vi.

Oxford, Sketch of, Plate XXIV.
Oxford (Earls of), Arms of, Plate XI.
Oxfordshire, 33; Forests in, 33.

Parliament, Burgesses of the, x, 62–64.
Pearson's (Dr.) remarks on the difference between the reputed and measured miles, x.
Pembroke (Earls of), Arms of, Plates IV., VII., XIII.
Pembrokshire, 56; Forests, 56; Castles, 56.

Radnorshire, 57; Forests, 57; Castles, 57.
Richmond (Earls and Duke of), Arms of, Plates XII., XVI.
Rivers, four principall, in England, 4–5.
Rochester, View of, Plate XIX.
Rutland, 38–39; Forests, 39.
Rutland (Earls of), Arms of, Plate XVI.

Salisbury, Sketch of, Plate XXI.
Salisbury (Earls of), Arms of, Plate X.
Scilly Isles, 60–61
Shires in England, 2–3.
——— in Wales, 3.
Shrewsbury, Arms of, Plate II.
Shrewsbury (Earls of), Arms of, Plate XI.
Shropshire, 43–44; Forests, 44; Castles, 44.
Sloane (Sir Hans), possessor of the "Description of England," v.
Smith, Arms of, Plate XVII.
Smith of Cuerdley, vi.
Smith (Jane), mother of William Smith, her death, vi.

Smith (Randle) of Oldhaugh, father of William Smith, vi; his death, vii.
Smith (Veronica), wife of William Smith, vi.
Smith (William), account of his life, v; made Rouge Dragon pursuivant, vii; list of his works, xi–xiv; list by himself, xv.
Somerset (Earl and Dukes of), Arms of, Plate XII.
Somersetshire, 18–20; Forests in, 20; Mores, 20.
Sorlingues, Isles of, 60–61.
Southampton, Arms of, Plate I.
Southampton (Earls of), Arms of, Plate VII.
Stafford, Sketch of, Plate XXVI.
Stafford (Earls of), Arms of, Plate XIII.
Staffordshire, 42–43; Forests, 43; Castles, 43.
Stonehenge, View of, Plate XXII.
Stuckley's (William) View of London, ix.
Suffolk, 27–28.
Suffolk (Earls and Dukes of), Arms of, Plates IV., XV.
Surrey, 11–12.
Surrey (Earls and Duke of), Arms of, Plate VI.
Sussex, 9–11; Forests, 10–11.
Sussex (Earl of), Arms of, Plate XXII.
Swenter, Arms of, Plate XVII.

Vales in Dorcetshire, 18.

Wales, 53–59; Shires in, 3.
Wales (King and Princes of), Arms of, Plates VII., VIII.
Warren and Surrey (Earls of), Arms of, Plate VI.
Warwick, Arms of, Plate I.
Warwick (Earls of), Arms of, Plate VI.
Warwickshire, 37–38.
Westmoreland, 51; Forests, 51; Castles, 51.
Westmoreland (Earls of), Arms of, Plate XIII.
Wight, Isle of, 60.
Wiltshire, 15–17; Forests in, 16.
Wiltshire (Earl of), Arms of, Plate IX.
Winchester, Sketch of, Plate XX.
Winchester (Earls and Marquis of), Arms of, Plate VIII.
Wonders in England, ix, 6.
Worcester, Arms of, Plate I.
Worcester (Earls of), Arms of, Plate IX.
Worcestershire, 36–37; Forests, 37.

York, Arms of, Plate II.
York (Duke of), Arms of, Plates II., XIII.
Yorkshire, 47–50; Forests, 50; Castles, 50; Abbais which sometime were, 50; Arms of, Plate II.

University of California
SOUTHERN REGIONAL LIBRARY FACILITY
Return this material to the library
from which it was borrowed.

5-5-93

D 000 011 349 8

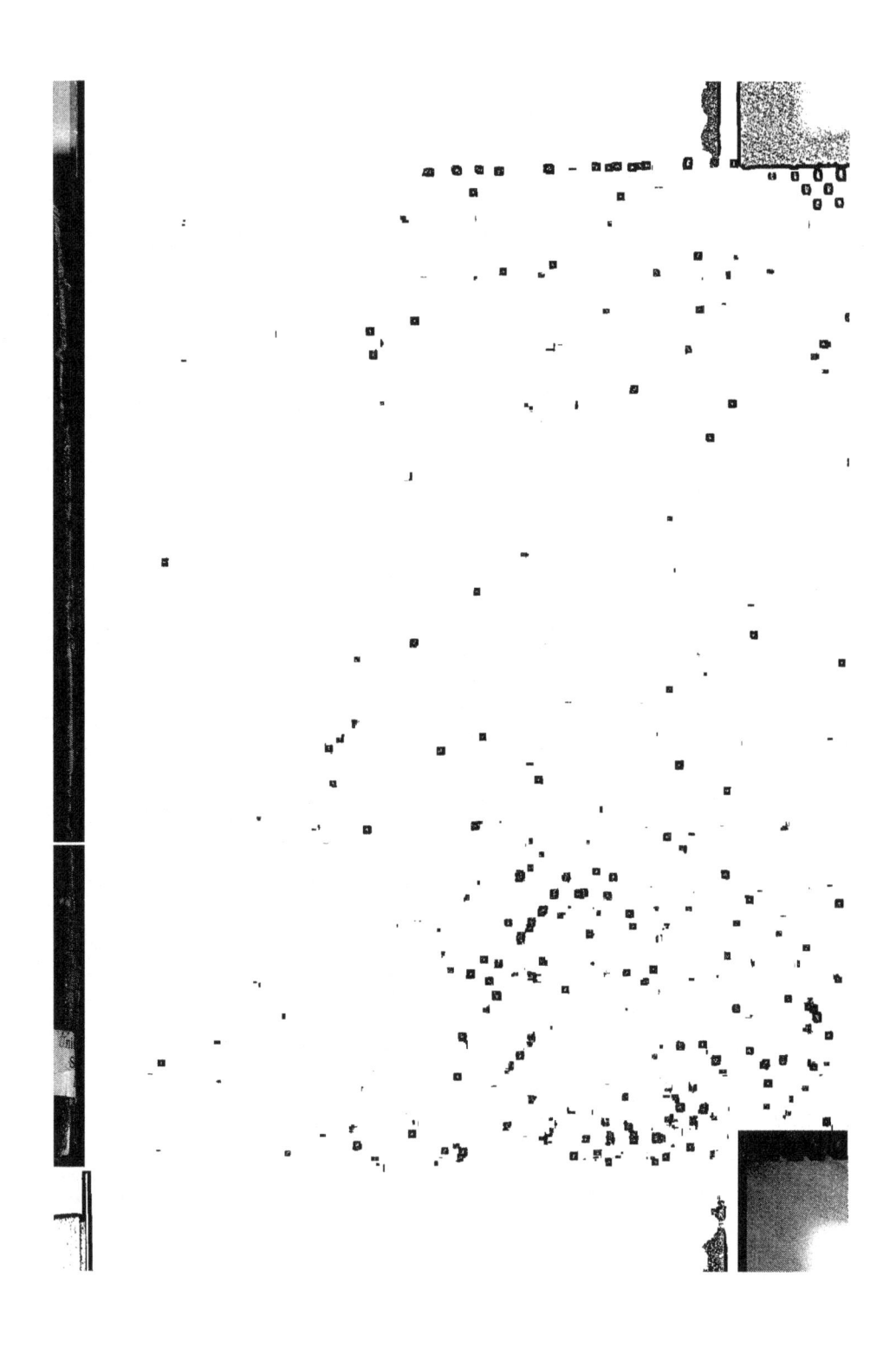